Endorsements

Overcoming an orphan mentality is often challenging for many today, yet Chad Waller uniquely addresses this in his book, "Sons...Overcoming An Orphan Mentality". With honesty and sensitivity he gives practical steps and biblical insight that sheds light and a pathway to healing. Chad is not a theorist, writing from the tower of research alone, but is a practitioner who has ministered to many over the years. I have personally experienced the heart of this message in the ministries and lives of those that Chad leads.

If you or someone you know struggles with fully understanding their identity as a son or daughter in Christ, this book will serve as a guide to help comprehend the fullness of what God, The Father has for each of us.

Doug Stringer
Founder / President
Somebody Cares America / International
Turning Point Ministries International
Author - In Search of A Father's Blessing

I have known Pastors Chad and Melinda since 1995, in many ways we have grown up into "sonship" together. I love how Chad writes about his relationship with the Father and the Holy Spirit's work of healing and deliverance in his life. God uses Pastor Chad as a powerful minister of freedom in other's lives because he is a "son who is free indeed" and he always gives the glory to the One who loved him first.

Endorsements

This book is a must read for every Christian and will be listed as recommended reading for those who attend the Healing Waters weekend, deliverance and healing ministry of He Cares for Me.

Marlene J. Yeo
Lead Pastor, Community Christian Fellowship
www.ccfhaverhill.com
Director Somebody Cares New England
www.somebodycaresNE.org
Director He Cares for Me
www.HeCaresForMe.org
Author - Where's God On Tuesday

-

Chad has been shaped by the beauty of Sonship that came from embracing God as a good Father. The greatest injustice is a heart left fatherless. Chad is bringing justice to the generations in his life message of Sonship. Keys for freedom, mindsets for true living, & an authentic heart are all found in this book. Enjoy, live, & share what you find here.

Eric Reeder
RISEmovement Inc., Leadership & Vision Coach.
www.wearethehopeful.com
Author - Generational Synergy

-

Pastor Chad's book on sonship is a must read. One more time, he hits it out of the park with unbelievable insights, rock solid truths, and allows us to see the real man behind the writing. I have great respect for this man of God. His love for the Father and his pursuit of understanding what it means to be a spiritual son comes through in every facet of his life. His home, relationships, leadership and pastoring are impacted greatly because he continues his pursuit in knowing his sonship. I love his openness to write from a place of pursuit rather than arrival and as he says in this book, "This is an amazing journey of discovery and recovery."

Whether they know it or not, this is the cry of every person alive, to know their Spiritual Sonship. Chad shows us that this is possible for all people, not just the churched. He reveals to us that God desires for all to know this truth and to live in it.

This book is not just words, but It's revelation that a man has and is walking through. I can get behind that all-day long. It is my belief that every person on the planet needs to read this more than once. So, whether you are a strong believer in Jesus, or you are a once month attender, or you have walked away for whatever reason, or even if you don't believe in Jesus yet, this book is for you! The answer you may be looking for just may reside in this book as it guides you in knowing your Spiritual Sonship.

Mark Wargo
Lead Pastor, Cross Current Church
www.crosscurrent.tv
Author - Beyond Betrayal

Pastor Chad is a beloved son in whom I am well pleased. In this book he shares his heart; and he portrays the heart of Father God in a poetic and profound way. The chapters are full of Kingdom theology with the power to transform and set people free. In recent weeks I felt the Spirit of the Lord impress on me that there are many believers who drift aimlessly from church to church because an orphan spirit rules their minds. To that point, this book is a must read. Sons:

Endorsements

Overcoming An Orphan Mentality is valuable 21st century apostolic insight into the heartbeat of our Heavenly Father. I strongly endorse this work.

> Apostle Raffoul Najem
> Sr. Pastor CCF Ministries
> (One Church Many Locations)
> Founder & Administrator
> Community Christian Academy

"Pastor Chad Waller provides an engaging and insightful understanding of what it means to accept and embrace our roles as children of God. Being firmly rooted in scripture, but still easy to read, Chad provides us with what it means to walk as a son and daughter of God, how to walk in our rights as God's children, and how to identify ourselves within those rights and God's kingdom.

So often we identify ourselves as Christians, yet we also identify ourselves as other things, whether it is through our family and friends, our possessions, or our careers. Sons - Overcoming an Orphan Mentality shows us that we are created, and given the right as God's children, to be so much more.

Regardless of where you are in your journey with the Lord, if you struggle with what it means to identify as a child of God, or if you want to go further in what God has in store for you and your life, you should read this book."

Aaron Palmer, J.D.

Endorsements

"There are books that carry helpful information that can assist in bringing an intellectual framework. Then there are books that carry impactful revelation that can usher in a bandwidth of breakthrough. This is that kind of book. The message contained within these pages come from Chad's own personal experience and freedom. It is not theory, it is reality that invites the reader to break out of orphan tendencies and to dive into the depths of sonship."

Brian Orme
Founder, Kingdomstrate
www.iborme.com
Author - The Ascended Life

Sons

Overcoming An Orphan Mentality

by Chad E. Waller

© Copyright 2017 Chad Waller.

All rights reserved. Written permission must be secured from the publisher to use or reproduce any part of this book, except for breif quotations in critical reviews or articles. The use of short quotations or occasional page copying for personal or group study is permitted and encouraged.

Scripture quotations are from the ESV® Bible (The Holy Bible, English Standard Version®), copyright © 2001 by Crossway, a publishing ministry of Good News Publishers. Used by permission. All rights reserved.

"Orphan." Merriam-Webster.com. n.d. https://www.merriam-webster.com/dictionary/orphan (6 Feb 2017).

Strong, James. "Perfect." Strong's Expanded Exhaustive Concordance of the Bible. Nashville: Thomas Nelson, 2009. Print.

Strong, James. "Children." Strong's Expanded Exhaustive Concordance of the Bible. Nashville: Thomas Nelson, 2009. Print.

Scripture quotations marked MSG are taken from THE MESSAGE, copyright © 1993, 1994, 1995, 1996, 2000, 2001, 2002 by Eugene H. Peterson. Used by permission of NavPress. All rights reserved. Represented by Tyndale House Publishers, Inc.

Contact Information:

Waller-Hill Publishing, LLC
P.O. Box 493
Tenille, GA 31089
www.wallerhill.com

10 9 8 7 6 5 4 3 2 1

To all the spiritual orphans, some trapped in prisons of your own making, some broken down by religious obligation, others chained to failures of the past, but all looking for Father's love – He loves you more than you dare to believe!

Table Of Contents

Foreword	15
Introduction	17
1. Who Are The Sons Of God?	19
2. What Is An Orphan Mentality	27
3. How The Orphan Mentality Manifest	33
4. Biblical View of Orphan Mentality	39
5. Accepting Your Sonship Rights	49
6. Stages of Sonship	59
7. Like Father Like Son	67
8. Steps To Overcoming An Orphan Mentality	77
9. Sonship and Sin	87
10. Stories Of Those Who Overcame	95
11. No More Spiritual Orphans	113
12. Conclusion	119

Foreword

After attending Rhema Bible Training Center for two years I returned home to Central Georgia and began attending my mother's church. I heard Chad share about his recent experience at a prayer conference. I was amazed to hear the heart of this young man. I heard a heart that was devoted to God and determined to know Him more. Little did I know that this was the beginning of a life journey together. Now we have been married for more than thirty years and have raised six children and are now blessed to imprint on the lives of eight grandchildren.

In all these years I have observed Chad's life from the day to day in both the public and private arena. As Joshua was to Moses, hanging close as Moses interacted with God, so I feel I have been with Chad. I have heard the frustration, desperation, and adoration to Father, that reveal the heart of a man who desires to please God rather than man. And like Joshua, I have grown much in my own relationship with Father because of it.

In our years of ministry I have noted a series of themes. First it was about worship. I watched Chad's life begin to transform as he grew in understanding that worship was more than singing songs to God; he learned it was a lifestyle that released the song of deliverance sung by the Lord over his life. Next, the Lord added the revelation of grace that empowered him to live life as a victor in Christ rather than as a victim of his past. Last, but not least, Chad received a revelation of sonship and adoption. It produced a confidence in Father God that is unparalleled. It has caused a ripple effect that has impacted our family, our church, and others who will receive it.

Sons reveals the culmination of Chad's life journey to now. My life would not be what it is today apart from the revelation that I was born to be a child of God and to grow up into the fulness of all that sonship includes. I am probably more qualified than anyone to write the foreword to this book as I have been on this journey with Chad and have watched him walk out the things that he has written about. We have had the joy of being on this glorious, but sometimes very difficult journey together. Don't just read this book, hear the heart of your Father God calling you deeper into what you were always meant to be. We are sons!

Melinda Anderson Waller
Co-Founder and Lead Pastor, VC2
Tennille, GA

Introduction

I have often struggled with the idea that if I know something then surely others know it as well. I have found it to be one of the hardest points to deal with in any instruction I have ever undertaken. The issue of our sonship in the Kingdom of God is such a point.

When I was first saved in the early 1980's, I attended a church where the message of who we are in Christ was taught a lot. Though it took much exposure to this new thought for it to finally begin to produce change in me, it did! I began to awaken to understand I was a new man in Christ. Living that out has proven to be a lifelong pursuit.

It was during these first years, on July 6th, 1986, while studying a daily devotional that I first heard the Lord call me "son." It freaked me out a bit. God's son? How could I be God's son? There was only one begotten son, right? I couldn't be His son, and I knew I wasn't Jesus, so what in the world was He saying? Yet, I knew with all my heart, He had spoken to me. He said simply, "My son, from this day forward you will never be the same." I don't believe I was!

It took many years for the depth of that revelation to unfold in me. In fact, I would later discover the things I had studied, which at the time seemed so important, were not the true treasure of that day. It was simply having God call me His own that changed me forever. It impacted me deeply. I remember weeping, but I now know that I didn't have the framework to even begin to comprehend what was taking place.

Introduction

My purpose for writing this book is to share the revelation of sonship that has been unfolding in my heart and how it has manifested in my life over the past 30 years. I believe it is a beautiful and much needed understanding for the body of Christ. Father God did not save us to be slaves in His Kingdom, but has called us, as His sons, to come to His table and be with Him! It is time for the church to wake up to what we have been called to be. We are not orphans, we are sons!

1. Who Are The Sons Of God?

I believe God is bringing a shift in our thinking and setting things in order. It is a noble thought to want to serve God because He has saved you. I understand the fear of the Lord and the desire to be pleasing to Him. However, I think there is a much higher thought life that He desires us to rise up into. He wants us to walk in our true identity and to understand our sonship.

If we don't know who we are, we can be wrongly convinced of being someone we are not.

When Jesus was getting ready to leave the earth, He made a promise that He would not leave us as orphans, but would send us a comforter. He said He would send us a Spirit, God's Spirit, and we now know that HE is a Spirit of Adoption. Holy Spirit came to fulfill what Jesus spoke. He adopted us into God's family!

"And I will ask the Father, and he will give you another Helper, to be with you forever, even the Spirit of truth, whom the world cannot receive, because it neither sees him nor knows him. You know him, for he dwells with you and will be in you. "I will not leave you as orphans; I will come to you."
John 14:16-18

"For all who are led by the Spirit of God are sons of God. For you did not receive the spirit of slavery to fall back into fear, but you have received the Spirit of adoption as sons, by whom we cry, "Abba! Father!" The Spirit himself bears witness with our spirit that we are children of God, and if chil-

dren, then heirs—heirs of God and fellow heirs with Christ, provided we suffer with him in order that we may also be glorified with him ."

Romans 8:14-17

It is very important for us to understand what this adoption as sons means. This takes us beyond the mentality of just **sinners saved by grace** to **sons adopted into the family.** We were not saved just to serve, but adopted to reign! Sons gladly serve, but they are not just servants, they are sons, with rights and authority; not slaves made to serve, but sons who freely serve. This Spirit of adoption causes us to understand our sonship and He bears witness with our spirits that we are children of God. Holy Spirit reaffirms in our hearts that we are indeed God's sons.

"Now before faith came, we were held captive under the law, imprisoned until the coming faith would be revealed. So then, the law was our guardian until Christ came, in order that we might be justified by faith. But now that faith has come, we are no longer under a guardian, for in Christ Jesus you are all sons of God, through faith. For as many of you as were baptized into Christ have put on Christ. There is neither Jew nor Greek, there is neither slave nor free, there is no male and female, for you are all one in Christ Jesus. And if you are Christ's, then you are Abraham's offspring, heirs according to promise."

Galatians 3:23-29

Notice that Paul says that all who are in Christ Jesus are sons of God, through faith. This is the key. We are not claiming sonship in Father by any works we have done. We, by no means, claim to have earned a spot in His family or any right to sonship. This was not our doing at all, but it was God's heartbeat and passion fulfilled—to bring us into the family! We are in the family through Christ who loved us and gave His life for us. So all who are in Christ are sons of

1. Who Are The Sons Of God?

God. In Christ, we have rights and authority as sons. This is precisely what the Father sent Jesus to do, bring many sons to glory! He has adopted us into His family and filled us with His Spirit and we are now one in Him.

It is also important to note that in Christ, there is no distinction made between male or female. We are all one in Christ. Females should take no offense at being called sons of God. I don't feel that it is necessary to water down sonship by saying we are children of God or even sons and daughters of God. Sonship mainly speaks of our authority and inheritance, as well as our position in Christ, where we are all one. The same thought goes for men seeing themselves as part of the Bride of Christ. We in no way diminish our personal femininity or masculinity when we identify as who we are in Christ. So please bear with me when I refer to us as sons in Christ.

The need for us to understand our sonship cannot be overstated. It is a foundational point in any person's life. The need for fathers, and for sons to be grounded in a father's love, has never been more clear than in our society today. It has almost become commonplace when life coaching (counseling) someone to begin with the simply question of their relationship with their father. So much seems to be connected to this. When I see a young man lacking confidence, I assume immediately that there was little, if any, relationship with a father or father figure. I am seldom wrong with that assumption.

I want to be clear on this point. Just because someone grew up with a father in the house or in their life, does not at all ensure that they had a relationship with him. I have read studies that suggest a father in the home, whether he is engaged with the kids lives or not, is better than no father at all and does produce some results. I believe the point has been clearly demonstrated to me, and I would dare say to our society, that we desperately need fathers to help mentor young people.

This need is also seen in the church. We must awaken to our sonship and find our place with the Father. Only in truly knowing our sonship and relationship with Heavenly Father, can we be great earthly fathers and reflections of what Father God looks like. Again, this is such a need in the Church presently to help others discover who they are in Christ. So many need to know that in Christ we are the sons of God, and as sons, we are heirs to His kingdom.

"But we see him who for a little while was made lower than the angels, namely Jesus, crowned with glory and honor because of the suffering of death, so that by the grace of God he might taste death for everyone. For it was fitting that he, for whom and by whom all things exist, in bringing many sons to glory, should make the founder of their salvation perfect through suffering. For he who sanctifies and those who are sanctified all have one source. That is why he is not ashamed to call them brothers"

Hebrews 2:9-11

I am so glad that Jesus is not afraid to claim us as His own! By His death, burial and resurrection, He has brought us into the glory that He and the Father shared from the beginning. So all who are in Christ, who have accepted the finished work of the cross as their salvation and believe that what Jesus Christ accomplished by His death, burial and resurrection, have been adopted into the family of God. We are the sons of the Almighty God!

If at this point in reading this book you feel uncertain as to whether you can call yourself a son of God or not, ask yourself why. What is it that is keeping you from identifying yourself as God does? Why do you feel you cannot call yourself His son?

1. Who Are The Sons Of God?

I believe there really are only a few answers to this question. Maybe you are a believer in Christ who is just not comfortable with saying this or claiming this title because of some previous religious training that leads you to believe to the contrary. This is easily resolved with simply seeing truth throughout the scriptures. I trust by the end of this book, you will be all set. Another reason would be that you feel you are unworthy to make such a lofty claim, and that you feel simply being a sinner saved by grace better fits your situation. I feel your pain, but it simply isn't biblical to make such a claim. If you stick through the end of this book, I think you will find help as well.

The third reason I will address will need a solution in order for this book to have much meaning to you. It truly is simple, but at the same time, very complex. It will cost you your life. It will mean you surrender your will to His will. Yes, I mean salvation through grace by faith. If you have never received what Jesus has done for you as your salvation or never believed on Him for salvation, then this is the point where you really should do that. Why? Because if you haven't done that, then you cannot receive this sonship. You are still dead in your sins and trespasses, but Christ wants to raise you up to new life and to bring you into the glory of sonship!

At this point, you may want to know how you receive Christ. Is there a certain prayer you must pray or certain thing you must say? No, there really isn't. There is no sinner's prayer, though you may have heard this statement over and over. It bugs me a bit that many Christians think that there is. I simply want you to read the following passage from Romans, and respond. Come on, you can do it. You use your own words and cry out to Father God! He has loved you from the beginning with an everlasting love and sent His Son to save you and His Holy Spirit to adopt you into the family. Come on in!

1. Who Are The Sons Of God?

"For Moses writes about the righteousness that is based on the law, that the person who does the commandments shall live by them. But the righteousness based on faith says, 'Do not say in your heart, 'Who will ascend into heaven?'" that is, to bring Christ down 'or 'Who will descend into the abyss?' that is, to bring Christ up from the dead. But what does it say? 'The word is near you, in your mouth and in your heart' that is, the word of faith that we proclaim; because, if you confess with your mouth that Jesus is Lord and believe in your heart that God raised him from the dead, you will be saved. For with the heart one believes and is justified, and with the mouth one confesses and is saved. For the Scripture says, 'Everyone who believes in him will not be put to shame.' For there is no distinction between Jew and Greek; for the same Lord is Lord of all, bestowing his riches on all who call on him. For 'everyone who calls on the name of the Lord will be saved.'"

Romans 10:5-13

Please call on the name of the Lord, confess Him with your mouth, and trust in Him. He has done for us what we could not do for ourselves. And now He is offering you adoption into His family. Everyone who calls upon the name of the Lord will be saved!

God is setting us free from the orphan mentality.

Think About It:

What does it mean to you to go beyond the mentality of just being sinners saved by grace to sons adopted into the family of God?

_____
_____
_____
_____

1. Who Are The Sons Of God?

Further Study:

Look up the following scriptures and write down what they tell you about who you are in Christ? Colossians 2:9-10; 3:1-3, 2 Corinthians 5:17, Galatians 3:26

_____
_____
_____
_____
_____
_____
_____
_____
_____

2. What Is An Orphan Mentality

Let me first say that by using the term orphan I mean no disrespect to anyone who has lost a father and mother and found themselves literally orphaned. Understanding what orphans experience when they lose parents will help us understand what a person with a spiritual orphan mentality lives like. In this chapter we will look at what the orphan mentality is and then in the next chapter we will discuss how it manifest in our lives.

Merriam-Webster.com defines an orphan as *a child deprived by death of one or usually both parents. or as one deprived of some protection or advantage.* "Orphan." Merriam-Webster.com. Merriam-Webster, n.d. Web. 6 Feb. 2017. So an orphan is someone who is on their own or has no one to protect them, provide for them, comfort them or care for them. Often, natural orphans become wards of the state and may go from foster home to foster home, feeling as though they never really belong anywhere. Orphanages have historically been established to care for those who have had no place to go. I have interviewed people who have been orphaned to understand what they experienced. I can tell you that I see so many of the same feelings that orphans experience in the life of people in the church that have been saved but still live with an improper view of God as Father.

So for the purposes of this book, and our understanding of what God is setting the church free from, we will define a spiritual orphan as someone who feels they simply have no one to protect them, provide for them, comfort them or care for them. To make this clear, I am not addressing unsaved

2. What Is An Orphan Mentality

people who have never made a decision to follow Christ. I am speaking of those who have done so but still live as if God is somewhere far off and they live their lives in fear of displeasing Him and being punished for doing so. I am trying to identify the orphan mentality in the church (which I believe is rampant) and call the body of Christ to awaken to what has been given to us.

There is a difference in a mentality and a spirit. I don't plan to debate demonic influence, possession or whether a Christian can be oppressed. That is not the subject of this book. I simply don't believe that what most people deal with when it comes to the orphan mentality is demonic as much as it is a mentality or a way of thinking that is beneath who we really are in Christ. I do believe that it is important to explain to you why I have chosen to call it an orphan mentality and not an orphan spirit.

If you have a certain mentality, or way of thinking, simply finding the truth and accepting it can change the way you think. As we grow up, we have many things that we may think are true that change as our understanding changes. As kids, maybe you believed something that as an adult, with more understanding and life experience, you see differently. All of us have experience receiving information that changed the way we thought about something. I know that as I have grown in my faith I have had numerous mindset shifts. We are told to renew our minds by the washing of the water of the word. This is bringing ourselves into remembrance of what the Word of God says about us. Allow me to use a personal story to explain how mindsets or mentalities can change.

When I was a young child I had a difficult time with multiplication. We were memorizing the times table in school and I just didn't seem to be doing well with it. One day a teacher, trying no doubt to encourage me, told me that I just wasn't good at it and I should accept that I may never be. She went on to tell me how talented I was in other areas and that I should just focus on those. I so took it to heart that I never really excelled in math. I did average in that subject, while doing well in all others. In fact, my senior year in high school I transferred out of Trigonometry because I just couldn't pass it. By that point in my life I had begun to surrender to Christ and was attempting to trust Him with everything. I apologize if that sentence makes you uneasy but my conversion was not so cut and dry as I hear other people describe theirs. I can't tell you at exactly what moment or time I truly trusted Christ for salvation. You see, I was raised in church, knew all the stories and knew all about God but can't say I truly knew Him. It was in my last two years of high school that I started to get to really know God. This is when I began to pray and develop a relationship with the Lord.

One day as I was praying, I simply asked a question. "Why am I not good at math?" And Holy Spirit took me right back to that classroom, where as a child I had heard the words of a misguided teacher spoken to me. Again, I don't mean to represent her as evil, but it does give us pause to think about the words we speak over others. It was those words, "You will never to good at math," that came back so clearly to me that day. I had taken those words to heart and literally lived them.

I ask Holy Spirit to help me and to shift my mind to believe something different. I had been memorizing scripture and had recently learned Philippians 4:13. This had encourage me to believe that because I was in Christ and He was strengthening me I could actually do all things. I started telling myself that there was actually no reason that I could not learn math and that I had simply believed a lie. So, I enter college the summer after graduation and my very first class was a math class. I had something to prove.

2. What Is An Orphan Mentality

Let me make something very clear, I worked and studied hard that summer. Not only did I pass that summer semester of a college math class, I made the only A in the class. I had a complete mindset shift that summer. I went from being someone labeled as not able, to understanding that even if I had to work hard for it, I could do it! There was no reason that I could not except that I had believe that I could not. It was a mentality that I had accepted; a view of myself that was not true. As I received the truth and began to walk in it, things changed.

Honestly the list goes on. I didn't spell well. I struggled with dyslexia. I had a hard time paying attention. These were just some of the lies that I had allowed to limit me. As I began to renew my mind to what the Word said about me and found out who I was in Christ, my mentality about myself changed.

I believe mentalities can change as we embrace the truth. Again, we have to renew our minds to the truth. Life experiences, the words people have said about us, and the things we have spoken over ourselves have often shaped our mentalities into what we believe ourselves to be. Often, we have believed lies about ourselves. These are the things we have to let go of and allow the Holy Spirit to wash us and renew us to the truth!

"Do not be conformed to this world, but be transformed by the renewal of your mind, that by testing you may discern what is the will of God, what is good and acceptable and pefect."

Romans 12:2

There is a transformation that takes place as we renew our minds to what God says about us and it leads us into His will and purpose for us. This is exactly what happened in my life. As I began to understand who I was in Christ, and

2. What Is An Orphan Mentality

that my life was hidden with Christ in God, I began to find myself in Him. The things I had believed about myself began to change.

As I look back over the past 30 years I can see how God has been renewing my mind to the sonship I have in Him. I can look at so many messages, books and times of study that all worked together to bring me into a deeper understanding of God as my Father and my place of sonship in Him. I don't claim to have received the fullness of this revelation but as Paul said, I press on to make it my own! I can tell you I am so at rest in who my Father is and who He says I am!

It is difficult to describe what the orphan mentality is without talking about how it manifests, but we will look at that in Chapter Three. I only want to make sure here that we understand that the orphan mentality affects the way we think about God and the way we view Him. It is our refusal to receive what Jesus came to restore us to, and a denial of who are already are in Christ. We are sons, not slaves!

To be a spiritual orphan is to believe that God doesn't care about the mundane things in your life. It is to believe that you are on your own to make something of your life or to believe you have to make a way for yourself. Spiritual orphans do not find their care, protection, comfort or strength in the Father because they simply have no relationship with the Father. I do not mean to indicate they are not saved, as that is not mine to judge. I do, however, think that many believers live below their rights as sons of God.

Think About It:
What is an orphan mentality?

_____

_____

2. What Is An Orphan Mentality

Do you feel you have any mentalities or ways of thinking that are holding you back? If yes, be honest with yourself and write your thoughts here.

_____
_____
_____
_____
_____
_____

Further Study:

Romans 12:2 speaks of being transformed by the renewal of the mind. I suppose we all understand we do this with the Word of God. But how? Look up the definition of the word renew and see if it gives you any clues. It's good stuff!

_____
_____
_____
_____
_____
_____
_____
_____
_____

3. How The Orphan Mentality Manifest

There are many ways that the orphan mentality can manifest in our lives. Some are very subtle while others can almost paralyze our lives with fear and insecurities. I do not believe I can by any means exhaust all the ways here, but I will discuss what I have observed both in my life and in the lives of others that we have pastored.

One of the first things we need to break is any religious idea that we must work hard or do something to be accepted as a son of the Most High God! We, who are in Christ, are already one with Him. We are His inheritance, His beloved and we are the beloved of the Father. We are ONE!

"See what kind of love the Father has given to us, that we should be called children of God; and so we are."

1 John 3:1

You must settle the goodness of Father and His acceptance of you. The Father's amazing love has brought us into a place of sonship. John says that we are sons, not that we will be or that we are becoming. We already are the sons of God!

A very interesting thing happened one day during a time of corporate prayer at our church, VC2. Our granddaughter, who was in attendance, was running around worshipping while prayer was going on. She participates in her way and doesn't always find it necessary to sing the song that the worship leader may be be singing, but give her a break, she was only 3 at the time.

3. How The Orphan Mentality Manifest

On this day the leader was singing "Good, Good Father" while Libby was running around singing at the top of her lungs "Let it go! Let it go!" Over and over again she sang just these lines. (I apologize that I now have gotten that song stuck in your head.)

At first, as she sang that song, I only thought of how cute she was while she did it. Then it struck me, this little prophet was declaring a great truth. Some of us need to let go of how we have seen the Father. He is a good, good Father. That's just who He is!

This sonship is received simply through our belief in Christ and receiving from what Christ has done for us. It is our belief that brings us into sonship, NOT WORK! It is not by the abundance of our spiritual activity, but simply trusting that what Christ has done for us is enough. Orphans, believe it or not, often become fiercely independent when they feel that they have no one to run to. While sons are interdependent, knowing they have a Father who loves them and has adopted them into His family.

I think it is vital to point out what would seem like a very obvious point—you cannot adopt yourselves as a son, a Father must do that! This was not your doing. The Father adopted us, we didn't adopt Him! He brought us into His family!

"I mean that the heir, as long as he is a child, is no different from a slave, though he is the owner of everything, but he is under guardians and managers until the date set by his father. In the same way we also, when we were children, were enslaved to the elementary principles of the world. But when the fullness of time had come, God sent forth his Son, born of woman, born under the law, to redeem those who were under the law, so that we might receive adoption as sons. And because you are sons, God has sent the Spirit of his Son into our

hearts, crying, "Abba! Father!" So you are no longer a slave, but a son, and if a son, then an heir through God."

Galatians 4:1-7

Orphans feel they must work to earn their keep. They work for a place of acceptance and not from a place of acceptance. There is a huge difference. When you know your acceptance with the Father, you will serve Him gladly, but not because you are trying to earn something. Sons serve Father, but they do it in love. Orphans serve, hoping for praise or reward, and if they do not receive it, they are often hurt or dejected.

Someone with an orphan mentality sees God as a master while someone with an understanding of sonship sees God as a loving Father. Orphans strive for praise, approval and acceptance of man. They are very insecure and have a huge need for approval, much as a young child would as they are growing up. A son, who knows his place in the Father's heart, understands he is totally accepted and is at rest in the Father's love and grace.

For example, when my kids were younger, I expected them to need my attention and even my approval. They craved it, as young kids do as they are growing and developing. Often, I would be serenaded with the sounds of "Daddy watch me" or "Look what I can do!" With five kids there was always something new to see. However, as they grew up, their need for me to approve of them diminished. As they matured physically, emotionally and even spiritually, their need for me to approve of their actions and behavior became less and less. In fact, I remember noting at one point that my son was so certain of my approval of him, and of my love for him, that he had no fear of my disapproval. Someone who struggles with an orphan mentality feels that they can never do enough to please God and will work continually just hoping to make Him happy.

3. How The Orphan Mentality Manifest

A person who has an orphan mentality will struggle with self-rejection from always comparing themselves to others. It will often produce a very negative attitude when they feel they are treated poorly. While a son is usually more positive and affirmed knowing that they have great value to their Father-having no need to earn acceptance, but knowing they are freely accepted in Christ.

Feeling alone in a room full of people and feeling that no one cares for you shows a sign of an orphan mentality. Orphans deal with abandonment. It is often an overarching theme of their lives. This produces much anxiety and stress in them. When we are plagued with these feelings, truly nothing anyone says can change how we feel. We will not find freedom until we deal with the orphan mentality and renew our minds to the truth.

Fear of man is part of the orphan mentality. Fear of man is when we are constantly aware of what others think about us or how they perceive us. We can live in fear when we don't understand the full rights we have as sons. Fear comes from the place of not understanding our Father's goodness. We fear what people will do to us, or think of us. We fear having lack. We fear the future. All of this stems from an orphan mentality.

There may be many other ways that the orphan mentality manifests, but I am sure you get the idea. If I could sum it all up, orphans feel abandoned! To me, this is an amazing point, because it is the very thing that Jesus thought was important to address before He left the earth. Remember that Jesus promised He would not leave us as orphans! That was His promise to us, that we would not be alone in this, but there would be help. When you have an orphan mentality you feel you are on your own and nobody cares. This simply isn't true, our Savior has sent a comforter who cares for us!

3. How The Orphan Mentality Manifest

"And I will ask the Father, and he will give you another Helper, to be with you forever, even the Spirit of truth, whom the world cannot receive, because it neither sees him nor knows him. You know him, for he dwells with you and will be in you. "I will not leave you as orphans; I will come to you."
John 14:16-18

Here we see it clearly stated that we will not be left as orphans. Yet, it seems to me, many live with the orphan mentality. It is time for the sons of God to arise to their place of authority and to find their place at the Father's table!

If the Lord is your Shepherd, then you are not neglected, alone or abandoned!

Think About It:
Do you identify with any of the things spoken of in this Chapter? How has an orphan nature tried to find place in your life?

_____
_____
_____
_____

Further Study:
What other scriptures help us understand that it is not by our works that we have become sons of our Father God? (Hint: Look at Ephesians 2:9 and Romans 8:3)

_____
_____
_____
_____

4. Biblical View of Orphan Mentality

"For all who are led by the Spirit of God are sons of God. For you did not receive the spirit of slavery to fall back into fear, but you have received the Spirit of adoption as sons, by whom we cry, 'Abba! Father!' The Spirit himself bears witness with our spirit that we are children of God, and if children, then heirs—heirs of God and fellow heirs with Christ, provided we suffer with him in order that we may also be glorified with him."

Romans 8:14-17

I think this is a very important point because it takes us beyond the mentality of just being **sinners saved by grace** to **sons adopted into the family**. You were not just saved to serve but adopted to reign! Sons gladly serve but they are not just servants, they are sons, with rights and authority! They are not slaves made to serve but sons who freely serve!

Notice that Paul makes a clear distinction between slavery and sonship, declaring that the sons of God are led by the Spirit, but those trapped in religious slavery are driven by fear. Sons don't serve the Father out of fear. It seems to me that much fear based teaching has been peddled by the church to keep people under a religious system of bondage. Yet, we are taught in 1 John that perfect love cast out fear.

We see this picture in the parable of the Running Father (also known as the parable of the Prodigal Son) when the son returns home simply asking to be a servant, but the father has no desire to make his son a servant. He has only one thought—totally restoration back to his place as a son!

4. Biblical View of Orphan Mentality

Simply amazing to me. He just wanted to restore him back to his rightful place. He asked no questions nor did he hold anything against him. This is a beautiful picture of grace. Yet, I see the orphan mentality stronger in the brother who stayed home than the one who ran away and squandered his inheritance. Allow me to explain.

> *"And he said, 'There was a man who had two sons. And the younger of them said to his father, 'Father, give me the share of property that is coming to me.' And he divided his property between them."*
>
> *Luke 15:11-12*

Notice that the father divided his property between them! This is so important that we get this. The older brother was given his property. In fact, because the Father had done this, he practically owned nothing now. He had given his property to his sons! The older son would have most likely received a larger portion of the property as his inheritance. He already had all he needed, however what he truly needed was a heart change, better said, a mindset shift! He saw himself as a servant in his father's house, not an owner or joint heir! He already had rights as a legal owner of all he needed, but he protested when the father honored his brother, whom he viewed as an ungrateful traitor. Don't miss this point. The older brother had more than enough to do whatever He wanted to do but was angry with his father for not doing something for him.

The older brother had remained faithful to the father. He had worked and done his part to serve the best he knew how. He got angry and accused his father of not caring for him because he had not done for him what he felt he deserved. This is so much the orphan nature. He felt he was not being treated fairly and deserved better. Again, he already had it within his means to host whatever parties he desired. He was a wealthy man because his father had provided all that

4. Biblical View of Orphan Mentality

he needed. He was simply blinded to what was already his. He was striving to please his father instead of enjoying his relationship and exercising his own authority.

Father God wants you totally restored back to your place as a son!

Sons don't strive. There is a feeling I have dealt with in my times of walking with the Lord, and the simple term for it is striving. It is an internal pressure that would make me feel as though I was not doing enough for the Lord or that I was not doing enough to be holy or acceptable. I had to learn that sons are lead not driven; the enemy drives, Holy Spirit leads.

Sons are led! Orphans are driven! It amazed me to see that to be led means to bring or to carry. I really believe we must see the difference between being led and being driven. There is no peace in being driven, while there is much peace in being led. The Spirit of God leads us to where the heart of God needs us to do the will of God that He has prepared for us to accomplish. In fact, the only scripture that truly speaks of striving encourages us to strive to rest!

So how do we choose not to strive but to rest in the finished work of the cross? How do we choose to be led and not driven? It is only by getting to know the peace of God and allowing it to rule and reign in our lives.

"And let the peace of Christ rule in your hearts, to which indeed you were called in one body. And be thankful."
Colossians 3:15

There is a story in the Old Testament that also clearly portrays an orphan mentality. It happens after David becomes king of Israel and he remembers the covenant that he entered into with Jonathan, King Saul's son, and he asks if there is anyone left of Saul's house that he may show kindness to. He is informed that Jonathan has one son still alive.

> "And David said, "Is there still anyone left of the house of Saul, that I may show him kindness for Jonathan's sake?" Now there was a servant of the house of Saul whose name was Ziba, and they called him to David. And the king said to him, "Are you Ziba?" And he said, "I am your servant." And the king said, "Is there not still someone of the house of Saul, that I may show the kindness of God to him?" Ziba said to the king, "There is still a son of Jonathan; he is crippled in his feet." The king said to him, "Where is he?" And Ziba said to the king, "He is in the house of Machir the son of Ammiel, at Lo-debar." Then King David sent and brought him from the house of Machir the son of Ammiel, at Lo-debar. And Mephibosheth the son of Jonathan, son of Saul, came to David and fell on his face and paid homage. And David said, "Mephibosheth!" And he answered, "Behold, I am your servant." And David said to him, "Do not fear, for I will show you kindness for the sake of your father Jonathan, and I will restore to you all the land of Saul your father, and you shall eat at my table always." And he paid homage and said, "What is your servant, that you should show regard for a dead dog such as I?" Then the king called Ziba, Saul's servant, and said to him, "All that belonged to Saul and to all his house I have given to your master's grandson. And you and your sons and your servants shall till the land for him and shall bring in the produce, that your master's grandson may have bread to eat. But Mephibosheth your master's grandson shall always eat at my table." Now Ziba had fifteen sons and twenty servants. Then Ziba said to the king, "According to all that my lord the king commands his servant, so will your servant do." So Mephibosheth ate at David's table, like one of the king's sons. And Mephibosheth had a young son, whose name was Mica. And all who lived in Ziba's house became Mephibosheth's ser-

4. Biblical View of Orphan Mentality

vants. So Mephibosheth lived in Jerusalem, for he ate always at the king's table. Now he was lame in both his feet."

2 Samuel 9:1-13

Notice the response that Mephibosheth has when he is brought to King David. He is in fear for his life and we can only imagine what he is thinking the King wants to do to him. When the king tells him what he actually wants to do for him, he responds in disbelief and even calls himself a dead dog, wondering why the king would dare show him kindness. Almost in the same manner as the loving father in the parable Jesus told, King David pays no attention to Mephibosheth but instead, focuses only on restoration. He is simply interested in restoring all that is rightfully his.

This story is so full of grace, mercy, love and sonship. King David gave Mephibosheth a place at this table. He brought him out of a place of hiding and gave him a place of authority at the king's table. At the end of this passage, we are reminded that Mephibosheth was lame in both his feet. This happened when the kingdom was given to David and people who were of the house of Saul were fleeing and Mephibosheth's nurse dropped him while escaping. He was lame, in hiding, full of fear, and living like an orphan. How could he feel he had any right at the king's table?

His right to be at the table of the king had nothing to do with him and everything to do with covenant. When David asked if there was anyone that he could show kindness to for the sake of Jonathan, it was because of the covenant that he and Jonathan had entered into. So it was not earned by any descendants but it did belong to them. They did nothing to earn it. David says he wants to show the kindness of God. The word kindness here means covenant loyalties. Again, Mephibosheth did nothing to deserve this. He is only receiving the benefits of a convent into which he had been brought!

4. Biblical View of Orphan Mentality

We must understand we are much like this lame descendant of Jonathan. We did nothing to earn a place at the Father's table, however we are invited there because of the covenant that Jesus entered into with the Father. Our invitation to eat at the Father's table and to be His sons is completely based on what Jesus did and not anything we have done. Many of us identify with Mephibosheth's feeling that he was a dead dog and deserved no kindness from the king. I am so grateful that Father shows kindness because He is a God who keeps covenant and shows mercy. He is a loving Father who has made a way that His sons could rule and reign with Him forever!

You may feel that you are lame and unable to fulfill your place as a son. I would suggest to you, just as both the Loving Father in Jesus parable and King David in this story refused to listen to the unwarranted excuses of the orphan mentality from these two, so Father God is not interested in listening to the reasons you present for not being worthy to be called a son. You have been adopted into the family of God. This is not your doing, but is the work of a loving Heavenly Father who has sent His Spirit—the Spirit of adoption by which we cry, "Abba! Father!"

The battle seems to have always been about sonship and relationship. Adam and Eve were created for relationship with Father and I believe the enemy hated that relationship and did everything he could do deceive them into believing they were missing something. He succeeded, at least for a season, in bringing mankind down to a lower level where they forfeited their place with Father. Jesus came to seek and save that which was lost—relationship with the Father. He came to reveal the Father to us and to bring us back into sonship. That is why I say the battle has always been about sonship.

I believe there is still an amazing battle raging and the

enemy does not want sons to find their place in the Kingdom of their Father. Instead, the enemy desires that we would live our lives struggling to be good little Christians, thinking we must work hard to please our Father, never understanding our authority and our right to reign in life. He wants our lives to be riddled with the struggle to free ourselves from sin and doesn't desire for us to ever truly believe that Jesus has dealt with it.

The church has majored in teaching against sin as if overcoming sin is the pinnacle of our lives. When the truth is, Jesus already did!

Jesus overcame sin for us and invited us into His freedom. Sons find freedom in knowing the truth while orphans strive to find acceptance and approval by their actions. Sons grow in an understanding of the grace in which they stand and allow grace to teach them how to live upright, godly lives, even in the present darkness of this world. Grace frees us from sin, not to!

We cannot be saved by our works nor can we find acceptance with the Father by our works. Yes, we do good works because we love being a part of Father's Kingdom and giving ourselves to the work of the Lord. Good works flow from that place of love, not obligation. In fact, He prepared good work for us to do and as faithful sons we love serving Him. We actually co-labor with the Lord in extending His Kingdom on earth.

"For I consider that the sufferings of this present time are not worth comparing with the glory that is to be revealed to us. For the creation waits with eager longing for the revealing of the sons of God. For the creation was subjected to futility, not willingly, but because of him who subjected it, in hope that the creation itself will be set free from its bondage to corruption and obtain the freedom of the glory of the children of

4. Biblical View of Orphan Mentality

God. For we know that the whole creation has been groaning together in the pains of childbirth until now."

Romans 8:18-22

Even creation is longing for the sons of God to rise up and be what they have been called to be. In the glory of sonship revealed, creation will find freedom from the bondage that it was subjected to because of the fall. This is so powerful to me. As we find our places as sons and rise up, creation gets its glory back! We must rise as sons of God throughout the earth!

All creation is waiting for us to find our place at Father's table!

Think About It:

What stands out most to you in the story of David and Mephibosheth?

_____
_____
_____
_____
_____
_____
_____

Do you struggle at all with being restored back to your rightful place as a son of God? If so, in what ways?

_____
_____
_____
_____
_____
_____

4. Biblical View of Orphan Mentality

Further Study:

Read Ephesians 2:10. What does it tell you that God has already prepared for you?

_____
_____
_____
_____
_____
_____
_____
_____
_____

5. Accepting Your Sonship Rights

Sons have rights, so as sons of God it would stand to reason that we have rights. We must understand these rights if we are to extend the Kingdom of our Father. If you do not know what your rights are, you can be convinced of things that are not true. So what are our rights as the children of God and what has been afforded to us?

"For all who are led by the Spirit of God are sons of God. For you did not receive the spirit of slavery to fall back into fear, but you have received the Spirit of adoption as sons, by whom we cry, "Abba! Father!" The Spirit himself bears witness with our spirit that we are children of God, and if children, then heirs—heirs of God and fellow heirs with Christ, provided we suffer with him in order that we may also be glorified with him."

Romans 8:14-17

Looking again at these passages in Romans 8 shows us that we, as sons of God, will be led by the Spirit of God. I believe this is one of the most amazing rights and honors that we could have as God's sons. He has adopted us with His Spirit, the Spirit of adoption, and has filled us with that same Spirit to be for us a comfort and a guide. We can see that being led by the Spirit of God is an amazing privilege for us. Again, Jesus promised He would not leave us as orphans. **We are not alone!**

So if we are not alone, but have Holy Spirit as a leader and a guide in our life, then we can expect Him to help us daily. We can expect, as sons of God, to be led by the Spirit

5. Accepting Your Sonship Rights

of God. We can trust that when we are not sure what to do, Holy Spirit will lead us, because this is a sonship right and an awesome privilege. When we ask Him to lead, guide and direct us, we do so with the knowledge that we are not begging Him to do something for us that He is not sent to do or more than willing to do. It is our right to have His help in life. In fact, Paul says that being led by the Spirit of God is a mark of sonship.

Also in this passage we are told that since we are children of God then we are heirs with Christ. Simply put, this means that in Christ we have an inheritance. We are co-heirs with Christ. This is mind blowing to me! We aren't just saved, we are adopted as sons, and given a share of the inheritance and reward of Christ; though the enemy would love to convince me that I have no right to share in the reward of Christ. The fact remains that this was the plan of God all along. He has brought me into the family. He did not adopt me to fall back into fear or for me to be a slave. He adopted me to be a son—His son!

The last part of this passage in Romans says something that could possibly cause people to think that we must work to be sons. It would seem that we are heirs as long as we do what is necessary to be faithful and we will only be glorified if we remain faithful. If this is how you view it, then I strongly urge you to remain faithful and work hard. However, I think this has a completely different understanding.

I am a son, adopted by Father, and this was not my idea, but His, and the one who started this work will be faithful to complete it. I don't believe he has set a condition here on my sonship. So what then is this suffering with Christ in order to be a joint heir with Him in the Father? We suffer with Him when we identify as sons, are persecuted by the world and as we fight with ourselves to believe we belong to God. Jesus told us that the world did not recognize Him and they would not know us either.

> *"See what kind of love the Father has given to us, that we should be called children of God; and so we are. The reason why the world does not know us is that it did not know him."*
> 1 John 3:1

I believe that much of this suffering with Christ is standing for what is righteous, even when it is not popular. It is doing the right thing even when it is the hard thing. When we identify with Christ, and share the good news of the gospel, even at the chance of complete rejection or being put down for simply believing in God, we suffer. The fear of being rejected for what we believe is a huge struggle for many. To stand in your place as a son of the Most High God, even when the world does not understand, is to open yourself up to persecution. We can be of good cheer though, because the world also did not recognize Jesus. However, when He is revealed to the world, who we are will then be made clear!

I want to address the issue of trying to prove who you are and the trap that it will be in your life. Please hear this, **you don't have to prove anything to anyone**. I do not make that statement in a hard way nor does that thought give you permission to be mean to anyone. I am simply saying that trying to prove who you are to someone is part of the orphan mentality and it reeks of self-promotion. Learn to be who you are and diffuse the fragrance of Christ everywhere you go. Let the river of living water flow through you to bring refreshing and healing to others. When the glory of the Father is flowing through you, there is no need to prove anything to anyone.

It seems some people work so hard to convince others of who they are because they are simply not sure of themselves. They feel that if others can see what the Lord has done in them, then it makes it more legitimate and they find com-

5. Accepting Your Sonship Rights

fort in being seen as spiritually mature. Often, we are really just trying to convince ourselves of who we are. Even Jesus Christ, when questioned by Pilate about His identity simply replied, "You have said so." He did not argue with him and had nothing to prove to Him because He, Jesus, knew who He was! You must know who you are. It is here that we see another point of our sonship rights—obscurity!

Jesus said that the one who seeks to find His life will lose it, but the one who loses his life will find it. When we fight to prove who we are or fight for our own rights, seeking to establish our own kingdoms, we completely miss what Jesus taught us. We are here to glorify and honor God; to be a part of extending His kingdom, not build our own. In doing this, we often find that we are forced into obscurity to serve the least, the lost and the broken, much like Jesus did. I am concerned that popular Christianity sometimes makes it sound like we will all serve in the spotlight and be famous. I know that I think very practically, but I simply do not even see how this is possible. Big names and huge careers in the religious establishment are not the reason Jesus died on the cross. He died to raise us up to new life! He died to bring **MANY SONS TO GLORY**!

1 John 3:1 does not say we are becoming the sons of God, or that we will one day be the sons of God, but clearly and simply states that we are now! I feel this is very important for us to accept. We are the sons of God, even though the enemy hates it and religion fights this knowledge, it is who we are. We have to rise up into our true identities as sons and walk in this revelation in order to be involved with our Father's business. We must first be convinced that we are sons of God, and then in that complete awareness of what Jesus Christ has done for us, we rise to be who we are called to be.

Growing up, I never knew the rights we had as believers. I am not suggesting that it wasn't taught, maybe it was, but

5. Accepting Your Sonship Rights

I never understood. It wasn't until I surrendered my life to Christ in my teenage years that I begin to understand that we had rights as children of God. It was then that a whole new world was opened to me. This is when I began to understand that we were not simply sinners saved by grace but sons saved to reign with our Father. Let me clearly state that this is when it began. It was a long journey and quite a process.

I remember that my mother had gone to a convention of a nationally known speaker and she came home with some information I had never heard concerning our authority and rights as believers. She started sharing with the family things she had learned and I must admit it was foreign to me. I had never heard that my words had power. I didn't know that we had been given authority to declare things nor that we were commissioned to continue doing the things that Jesus had done while He was on earth. As we began to dig deeper into the Word of God and discover new things about the power of Holy Spirit, everything changed! It was more than a paradigm shift; it was a complete transformation. My heart was awakened to so much more than I had known.

It was in 1986 that I first heard God call me Son, as I explained in the introduction of this book. It was there in my apartment, before Melinda and I married, that I heard this. The journey into understanding what He said that day has been a long one. I was afraid to call myself His son because I had no understanding of what it meant. I did not want to say or do anything that was wrong or that would grieve Holy Spirit, but I knew what I had heard that day. It was many years later that the significance of that day was made clear to me.

If we are ever going to understand the power that He desires us to walk in, it is vitally important that we accept our place in the Father's heart. Equally important, if we never understand our rights, we will live our lives as beggars and never fully walk in our rights as sons of God. He has provided so much for us that many of us are not walking in. He has brought us in by adoption and we are now part of Him and are now growing up to understand our Father's will.

Jesus spoke of being about His Father's business, or in His Father's house, in Luke 2:49 which brings me to another sonship right. We have the awesome privilege of being involved with our Father's business. Paul even explained it to the church at Corinth like this, **"For we are God's fellow workers..." 1 Corinthians 3:9**

We co-labor with Christ for Kingdom purposes. It's part of our coco rights or coco assignment. I have this written on my office wall to remind me. And yes, it is written on there, not a picture or a poster, but written in black marker on the wall along with numerous other scriptures and statements of faith! It says this, *"We have been co-crucified, co-buried, co-raised, and now we co-labor with Christ!"* I love coco!

What an amazing honor it is that we as sons of God are not just saved to laze around the Kingdom, but are invited into the family business of healing the sick, raising the dead, seeing the broken restored, seeing needs met and seeing the Glory of our Father flood the earth! We get to be a part of that. It's the family business! This is an incredible right and humbling honor. He has set us free, anointed us and appointed us to be a part of releasing His goodness to the earth. The hope of glory lives inside of us and hope is flowing through us to bring change. We literally are the freedom and the change that the world is waiting for. Christ in us, the hope of glory. However, we must awaken to what is inside and to what has already been done for us by Christ's death, burial, and resurrection. I must acknowledge my coco state!

5. Accepting Your Sonship Rights

As a young believer, I was praying one day and begging God to deliver me from something. I heard so loudly in my spirit, "Chad, I have delivered you." I began to argue with God because I had clear proof and plenty of evidence that spoke to the contrary. It seemed obvious to me that I was very much not free. At least my actions and habits testified a different story than what I heard God saying. So how could He say He had set me free?

My argument seemed to fall on deaf ears, much as the son who came running home to His father in Jesus' parable. He simply kept telling me He had already set me free. I eventually cried out for understanding. I don't remember if it was in that moment or if it took some time, but I finally understood some deep truth. I started seeing it in prayer and worship and I saw it through out the Word of God. I had been set free by the work of the cross, I simply did not know how to walk in that freedom. New revelation began to flood my heart. I already was as much of a son as I would ever be, but I had to grow up into that sonship.

I already was as much of a son as I would ever be, but I had to grow up into that sonship.

We must acknowledge who we are in the Father's family, through Christ Jesus who has grafted us in, before we can begin to understand and walk in the freedom available to us. You don't find the freedom and then believe; you believe and then you find the freedom. Believing brings us into the freedom of sonship! I had to trust the Word and what it said about me before I saw it manifested in me.

"But to all who did receive him, who believed in his name, he gave the right to become children of God, who were born, not of blood nor of the will of the flesh nor of the will of man, but of God."

John 1:12-13

5. Accepting Your Sonship Rights

Before I ever felt like a son, I had to understand that because I had received Jesus Christ and believed in His name, He had given me the right to be a son of God. I had to believe, even though I didn't understand it, that this was God's doing and it was His will, not the will of a man. I had to trust! It would take years for me to learn to walk in it and learn to live it out. I am still in this process—a lifelong process most likely.

I accept, and celebrate, that I am a son of God, led by the Spirit of God and I am an heir with Christ, sharing in His reward. I am ok with a life of obscurity as long as His glory is shining through me. As a son, I have been entrusted with power and authority to help in my Father's business and have been called to extend His Kingdom in this earth. He has brought me into His victory and given me freedom. I freely accept these sonship rights. I did nothing to deserve them or to earn them, but freely He has given these rights to me.

Think About It:

Do you struggle to believe that you can be lead by the Spirit of God?

___

What are some ways Holy Spirit can lead us?

5. Accepting Your Sonship Rights

Further Study:

If you know you have been adopted by Father God, then what are some of the rights you need to remind yourself that you have? Search the Word to find scriptures that confirm these rights.

_____
_____
_____
_____
_____
_____
_____
_____
_____

6. Stages of Sonship

There is a simple understanding that babies grow up to be toddlers, then move on into the childhood stage, then grow up to be teenagers, and eventually into adulthood. This is a natural process. Yet, we have all known someone that did not seem to follow the process well for one reason or another. I am almost certain you know someone, or either you are that someone, who has been asked when they plan to grow up. Just because the natural outward stages of life take place and your body goes from one level to the next, does not mean that your mental state will change. I have seen grown men act as though a child was trapped inside of them.

Let me be quick to say that being childlike and childish are two different things. I know Jesus said we have to come as children but I don't remember Him saying act childish, throw temper tantrums, always demand your way, and poop or pee wherever you please! Nope! I am most certain He expected us to grow up. When He spoke in Mark 10:15 of coming to the Kingdom as a child, He most certainly was speaking of childlike trust and faith.

Some people get stuck in a past stage of life because of trauma that occurred and seem to not want to progress beyond that. They may have full grown bodies, but their mental or emotional capacity may be way behind in development. One should not assume that because someone looks like a man that he knows how to act like one. I can personally testify that it took me many years of manhood before I stopped seeing myself as a little boy. Until I stopped seeing myself as a victim, I could not see myself as a man. I only saw a little boy being hurt, feeling rejected and alone—even in a crowd of people! I had grown up physically but not emotionally and I depended on other people to prop me up emotionally.

I will not write anymore here of my story, but you can read my book *Ash Sculpting 101: Learning To Live Emotionally Healthy In a Broken World* if you would like to understand more about becoming emotionally healthy. I cannot overstate the connection of emotional brokenness to the orphan mentality. You must allow God to heal you emotionally if you are ever going to be able to walk in the place of sonship that He has called you to.

If we get stuck at any place in our emotional development, we are most likely to live like spiritual orphans. We feel like we are abandoned there. Some live with the feeling that the world has moved on without them, while many have issues just coping with life. I often hear people complain of what they call "adulting" or being a grown up because of all the responsibilities and challenges that come with being an adult. This is part of growing up though, knowing what is required of you and what your responsibilities are as an adult. Paul spoke of growing up and putting away childish things.

"When I was a child, I spoke like a child, I thought like a child, I reasoned like a child. When I became a man, I gave up childish ways."

1 Corinthians 13:11

Someone with an orphan mentality struggles with giving up childish ways. They find it is easier to do what has always worked for them than to grow up and learn the right way to do things. Grown men having childish temper tantrums just look plain silly. Yet, we see this behavior often from people who use their emotions to manipulate others. I

6. Stages of Sonship

suppose the temper tantrums aren't any more silly than the silent treatment. All are meant to manipulate someone so we can get our way and are part of the childishness that we are expected to put behind us as we grow up.

We teach our kids, well let me restate that, we should teach our kids as they grow up how to become responsible and help them learn and grow through the stages of life. It is obvious that we do not expect the same things out of a 2 year old that we do a 16 year old. I would not ask a toddler to cut the grass, but would not hesitate to ask a teenager. I expect the older child to have the ability to do this task, but the younger is not even able to operate the machinery. So we see a natural progression in responsibility that correlates with the natural growth of a child. When I was a child I did childish things, but when I became a man I put away childish things.

We really should do a better job at teaching children how to deal with emotions as they are growing up. Simply telling a child to stop crying or suck it up, is not teaching them how to deal with their emotions. It actually teaches them to hide or shove them down deep inside, which is incredibly unhealthy. Part of growing up should be learning how to deal with our emotions in a healthy way.

On the morning of my 13th birthday I announced proudly to my mother, "Mom, things will change for me today and I will be acting differently from now on because today I become a teenager!" I have no idea what was in my mind, but it seems I felt back then that this was a cut and dry issue; childhood was over and teenage years were here! Oh that it were that simple or that easy. It isn't.

I am sure every kid has heard the sound of an adult's voice saying, "Aren't you a little old for that?" I know I have. Like recently when Melinda and I were at a park with our friends, Pastors Mark and Tracee Wargo, and I saw this thing there that was exactly like I used to play on as a kid. I call it a thing because I don't know what it is called. It is a big duck on a spring and kids hop on it and rock back and forth. Well I hopped right up on that thing, with quite more substantial girth than when I was a kid and that poor duck sank right to the ground! I mean I buried that duck. It was hilarious! Mark even took a picture of it. I get a text from time to time with that picture in it. I pray it gets lost somewhere.

Why do I share this story? Because I was doing something that day, just having fun and being silly but it quickly became obvious that I was too big for that thing that I used to do. It just didn't fit anymore. I only wish that it could be as apparent to us when we are acting emotionally out of sync with our age. Remember when we used to say as kids, "Act your age, not your shoe size?"

I think that we can assign levels of growth to each section of our development, though I know some of it is a generalization. There are a few clear boundaries and several rites of passage. There is a certain age most people get a learners permit to drive and then similarly a driver's license. Most kids graduate from high school around the same age. But these events do not ensure that a child will grow up. There must be proper physical, spiritual and emotional nourishment in order for someone to grow up in a healthy way.

I want to caution that when you get a revelation of being a son of God and begin overcoming the orphan mentality, do not be too hard on yourself. Allow yourself to grow and allow your mindsets to be adjusted to your new understanding. Renew your mind to truth and remind yourself who you are in Christ. You will see things begin to change. You will start to see yourself, your situations and your Father with different vision.

6. Stages of Sonship

"So put away all malice and all deceit and hypocrisy and envy and all slander. Like newborn infants, long for the pure spiritual milk, that by it you may grow up into salvation— if indeed you have tasted that the Lord is good."

1 Peter 2:1-3

Peter uses language of growing up spiritually here. Growing up into salvation doesn't mean you are not saved but means we grow up to understand what we are saved to. I believe many people know what they were saved from but not what they were saved to. Again, this is an area of childishness. When you are a child you don't always understand the way things work. When we came to Christ, or first surrendered our wills to Him, we most likely knew He was saving us from ourselves, our own pride, or maybe some particular brand of sin we were involved in, but we most likely didn't see clearly what He had saved us to do from the beginning. We grow up in our understanding of the Kingdom of God.

It is always interesting to me how kids think. They see things so differently than we do because of their level of understanding of how things work. I remember one day, when our kids were younger, they had asked to go and do something and I had to tell them it just wasn't in the budget and we could not afford to do that. I clearly remember our youngest child, Jordan, responding with a great solution. "Dad," she said, "Just go by that machine and put your card in that gives you money!" I had to have a lesson with her that money was only there and available to us if I had previously put it in. I am almost positive that she did not comprehend what I told her that day, but I am fully aware that now, as a college student, she clearly understands.

We grow up in our understanding of forgiveness, love, and selflessness. We grow in our knowledge of the Word and make decisions to relinquish our will to the will of Father. As we grow spiritually, we learn that living the Christ life is not about always about us but is about serving others. We learn to lay down our lives for others. We learn so much about the Kingdom by getting to know the King and growing in our understanding of His desires.

There is no shame in being a spiritual babe, but we should not stay there. Equally as true, being a toddler in the Kingdom of God and just learning how to speak Kingdom language is great, but we cannot stay there. We must drink the pure spiritual milk and grow up in this wonderful salvation that we have been brought into. All the way through the process of growing up spiritually, our desire should be to go to the next level. Our Father desires that we, as sons, grow into all that He has for us.

The writer of Hebrews addresses this issue in a pretty harsh way when he says this:

"About this we have much to say, and it is hard to explain, since you have become dull of hearing. For though by this time you ought to be teachers, you need someone to teach you again the basic principles of the oracles of God. You need milk, not solid food, for everyone who lives on milk is unskilled in the word of righteousness, since he is a child. But solid food is for the mature, for those who have their powers of discernment trained by constant practice to distinguish good from evil."

Hebrews 5:11-14

And Paul address these same matters with the Corinthian church and tells them this:

"But I, brothers, could not address you as spiritual people, but as people of the flesh, as infants in Christ. I fed you with milk, not solid food, for you were not ready for it. And even now you are not yet ready..."

1 Corinthians 3:1-2

6. Stages of Sonship

Ask Holy Spirit to help you identify where you are in the stages of spiritual growth and then refuse to stay there. Do something about it! Start moving forward and growing up into Christ! We are all in this journey together. Make a choice, as a true son of God, to move on into what Father is calling you to. Make the decision that you will not stay at the level of maturity that you are at. Let's all grow up!

Think About It:
What stage of sonship do you think you are at? Be honest with yourself.

_____
_____
_____
_____
_____
_____
_____
_____
_____

Further Study:
Read 1 Corinthians 3:1-9 and see who really brings the increase in our lives and helps us grow up.

_____
_____
_____
_____
_____
_____
_____
_____
_____

7. Like Father Like Son

This statement is usually used to describe someone who is very much like their earthly father and often is not a positive phrase. No greater thing could be said about a son of the Most High God. Yet this seemed to be a concept that the disciples had a hard time comprehending. Jesus came to reveal the Father to us and show us what a man filled with God looks like. He, without rhyme or riddle, declared if you had seen Him you had seen the Father.

One of my favorite conversations Jesus had with His disciples is concerning the subject of Father and how Jesus revealed Him. He stated plainly to see Him was to see Father and yet Philip still questioned Him.

"'Let not your hearts be troubled. Believe in God; believe also in me. In my Father's house are many rooms. If it were not so, would I have told you that I go to prepare a place for you? And if I go and prepare a place for you, I will come again and will take you to myself, that where I am you may be also. And you know the way to where I am going.' Thomas said to him, 'Lord, we do not know where you are going. How can we know the way?' Jesus said to him, 'I am the way, and the truth, and the life. No one comes to the Father except through me. If you had known me, you would have known my Father also. From now on you do know him and have seen him.' Philip said to him, 'Lord, show us the Father, and it is enough for us.' Jesus said to him, 'Have I been with you so long, and you still do not know me, Philip? Whoever has seen me has seen the Father. How can you say, 'Show us the Father'? Do you not believe that I am in the Father and the Father is in

me? The words that I say to you I do not speak on my own authority, but the Father who dwells in me does his works. Believe me that I am in the Father and the Father is in me, or else believe on account of the works themselves. 'Truly, truly, I say to you, whoever believes in me will also do the works that I do; and greater works than these will he do, because I am going to the Father. Whatever you ask in my name, this I will do, that the Father may be glorified in the Son. If you ask me anything in my name, I will do it.'"

John 14:1-14

The connection between doing the greater works and knowing Father God, understanding His heart and revealing Him, cannot be overstated. We see it here in the way Jesus answers Philip. Who does Jesus tell Philip is the one doing the works? The Father! Yes, through Him, Father is performing these works. Then Jesus tells Philip that because He is going to the Father, those that believe in Him will do not only these works, but even greater works! And all of it will be done for the glory of God!

Greater works are not as much about you as they are the Father's heart! It is God's desire to help people and He wants to do it through you!

I want to address an issue here that I know might be controversial for some and may be downright blasphemous for others. While others will see it is a simple thought and is easily seen in this passage. We should look like our Father. The same glory that Jesus and the Father shared from the beginning has been given to us. We are the temples of His Holy Spirit and we are filled with His glory. The hope of glory, Christ in us, shining through us in this dark world and flooding it with light, causes us to look like Father!

Now I know that you may be struggling with this thought as much as Philip did that day that Jesus said it. "Really, you look like the Father? Wow, I thought he would be so much more... um... heavenly! Or glorious?" Whatever the words were, it is obvious that Philip did not get it and I would dare say many don't get it now. I know this because most people I share this with immediately start telling me why this just isn't so. Is it possible that He, Jesus, was speaking of something deeper than physical looks. Are we so prone to think of the outward appearance that we missed something when He said, "If you've seen me, you've seen the Father?" I think we have missed it.

Jesus came to reveal Father God to us. He came in the flesh to show us Father's love. He taught of the Father's Kingdom and gave us principles of that Kingdom by telling us parables of what the Kingdom was like. He revealed to us how much Father cared for us. He was flesh and blood revealing spiritual things to us. He even told us that God is spirit and those that worship Him must worship Him in spirit and in truth. He was revealing to us what He, Father and Holy Spirit were like. Again, I don't think this is about how Father looks physically but about who He is, how He loves, and what His very essence is!

When you love, you look like your Father. When you give, you look like your Father. When you forgive, you look like your Father. When we are doing the things that Jesus taught us, we are unveiling Father and His love to this world. When others think we should curse someone, but we choose to bless, we look like our Father. When others give up on someone and say there is no hope and we still hold on to hope, we look like Father.

Jesus came, teaching things people had never heard, and by so doing, He revealed a side of Father God that had not been previously understood by all. He revealed the Father's love for the entire world. John 3:16 did bring us into a new understanding of the love of God.

7. Like Father Like Son

"For God so loved the world, that he gave his only Son, that whoever believes in him should not perish but have eternal life. For God did not send his Son into the world to condemn the world, but in order that the world might be saved through him. Whoever believes in him is not condemned, but whoever does not believe is condemned already, because he has not believed in the name of the only Son of God."

John 3:16-18

I often tell folks that the Bible does not state that God was so angry with the world, or that He was sick and tired of the world, nor that He hated the world. It clearly states that Jesus came because God so loved the world. Moreover, it states that God loved the world so much that He gave Jesus and whoever believes in Him can have eternal life! And then the next verse, John 3:17, that I rarely hear people quote, makes something else very clear. Jesus did not come to condemn the world, but to save it. Jesus came because of LOVE! Love came down to rescue us and bring us back into right relationship with our Father.

So Jesus revealed to us Father's love for us and His desire to have us restored back to our place of sonship in His heart. John, in Chapter 1, even states that all who believe are given the right to become the sons of God.

"But to all who did receive him, who believed in his name, he gave the right to become children of God, who were born, not of blood nor of the will of the flesh nor of the will of man, but of God."

John 1:12-13

Sons have their father's DNA, that's just the way it is. If you have been given the right, through Christ Jesus, to become a son of God, then whose DNA do you have? Notice John says this is not about flesh and blood nor the will of man. I know you are here physically by the will of a man and a woman. I know you are the product of a love relationship, or something that resembled one, but this is beyond that. He says our new birth into the Kingdom of God, is through God and by His will. So again, if we are spiritually God's kids then we have His spiritual DNA. We should look like our Father.

I am sure you are aware that the more you are around someone, the more likely you are to act like them. When our kids were growing up, they would sometimes come home from being around other kids and would try to use tactics that they had seen used in other homes. We would have to quickly acclimate them back to how things were done in our home. We know we are in this world but not of it. Yet if we are not careful, while living in it we can sometimes pick up traits from those who are of it. We can start acting like those around us, but you have been called to live a higher life. Holy Spirit convicts us of righteousness, or reminds us when we are not acting in a way that is like our Father!

We have been adopted into our Father's family for a purpose. He has filled us with His Spirit for a purpose. He has called us out of darkness for a purpose. We are representing and releasing His glory here on the earth.

"But you are a chosen race, a royal priesthood, a holy nation, a people for his own possession, that you may proclaim the excellencies of him who called you out of darkness into his marvelous light. Once you were not a people, but now you are God's people; once you had not received mercy, but now you have received mercy."

1 Peter 2:9-10

We were once spiritually alienated from the Father, separated by our own disobedience and sinfulness, but in Christ we have been adopted and brought close. We are now part of our Father's family. We are His children. Peter said that once, we had not received mercy, but now we have, and have been brought into sonship.

Jesus spoke about being sons of our Father who is in heaven. He makes a statement that has been the subject of much debate about us being perfect just as our Heavenly Father is perfect. The religious minded have a blast with this concept, often explaining away that this is impossible and that no Christian can be perfect.

"You have heard that it was said, 'You shall love your neighbor and hate your enemy.' But I say to you, Love your enemies and pray for those who persecute you, so that you may be sons of your Father who is in heaven. For he makes his sun rise on the evil and on the good, and sends rain on the just and on the unjust. For if you love those who love you, what reward do you have? Do not even the tax collectors do the same? And if you greet only your brothers, what more are you doing than others? Do not even the Gentiles do the same? You therefore must be perfect, as your heavenly Father is perfect."
Matthew 5:43-48

I don't use this scripture to by any means suggest that we have to do certain things or perform in certain ways to become sons of God. Jesus is trying to reveal to His disciples who the Father is and how we are to be like Him. He is debunking thoughts that religious leaders have taught and the loopholes they have created to allow the things they desire to get away with. He is teaching us to love like our Father loves; to love everyone just as our Father does.

Then He makes the statement, **"You must be perfect, as your Heavenly Father is perfect."** How can He possibly suggest that we be perfect and make no mistakes; that we never do anything wrong? This simply doesn't compute with our thoughts of humanity and would, at surface value, make us feel that based on this criteria, we cannot be true sons.

7. Like Father Like Son

The only problem is that the Greek word that is interpreted as perfect here is the word *teleios* and it does not mean perfect as we would think of perfect. It means mature, from going through the necessary stages to reach the end-goal. It means growing up one stage at a time to a place of functioning at full-strength, capacity or effectiveness. (*Strongs Concordance, 5046 teleios*)

The Strong's Concordance also explains that the best understanding of being perfect is the thought of the stages of life as seen in an old pirate's telescope, unfolding or extending one stage at a time to function at full-strength. As we grow, our understanding unfolds and we can see things more clearly. This is very much like Paul saying when he was a child, he spoke as a child, but when he grew up, he put away childish ways. As we grow up, our lives unfold so that we begin to understand what our Father understands in a more clear way. We begin to see love from His point of view. We begin to understand mercy, grace, faith and our Father's goodness toward us.

The simplest understanding of the word *perfect* is to be complete, and that is exactly what we are in our Father. We are complete. The Apostle Paul spent much time teaching the early church on our completeness in Christ. It seems it was obviously as needed then as it is today. The orphan nature pushes us to work to become more like God, when in fact, we were made in His image, filled with His Spirit, and have His very nature inside of us. Yes, I believe we need to grow up into it, but we are not trying to get something inside of us, rather we are growing up into Christ or into this great salvation that we have been brought into.

Jesus, when praying the beautiful words that John records in Chapter 17, says the most powerful thing about us being one with Him and the Father. I love His words written here. I have meditated often on these, trying to understand

7. Like Father Like Son

the depths of what He is saying. It is so obvious from His prayer that He was not thinking of bringing us in as servants or slaves in the Kingdom. He had something much more in His purpose for coming. It is almost mind boggling when Jesus asks the Father to make us one with Him the same way He and Father had been one from the beginning. Equally hard for us to comprehend is the fact that He says the same glory He and the Father had from the beginning, He wanted us to have. He speaks language of unity and oneness that the church simply hasn't comprehended. I want to close this chapter with that prayer. It is intense, it is long, but please take the time to drink it in and ask Holy Spirit to help you understand the words that Jesus is praying. Please know that this prayer, that Jesus prayed to the Father, will be completely answered!

"When Jesus had spoken these words, he lifted up his eyes to heaven, and said, 'Father, the hour has come; glorify your Son that the Son may glorify you, since you have given him authority over all flesh, to give eternal life to all whom you have given him. And this is eternal life, that they know you, the only true God, and Jesus Christ whom you have sent. I glorified you on earth, having accomplished the work that you gave me to do. And now, Father, glorify me in your own presence with the glory that I had with you before the world existed.

I have manifested your name to the people whom you gave me out of the world. Yours they were, and you gave them to me, and they have kept your word. Now they know that everything that you have given me is from you. For I have given them the words that you gave me, and they have received them and have come to know in truth that I came from you; and they have believed that you sent me. I am praying for them. I am not praying for the world but for those whom you have given me, for they are yours. All mine are yours, and yours are mine, and I am glorified in them. And I am no lon-

ger in the world, but they are in the world, and I am coming to you. Holy Father, keep them in your name, which you have given me, that they may be one, even as we are one. While I was with them, I kept them in your name, which you have given me. I have guarded them, and not one of them has been lost except the son of destruction, that the Scripture might be fulfilled. But now I am coming to you, and these things I speak in the world, that they may have my joy fulfilled in themselves. I have given them your word, and the world has hated them because they are not of the world, just as I am not of the world. I do not ask that you take them out of the world, but that you keep them from the evil one. They are not of the world, just as I am not of the world. Sanctify them in the truth; your word is truth. As you sent me into the world, so I have sent them into the world. And for their sake I consecrate myself, that they also may be sanctified in truth.

I do not ask for these only, but also for those who will believe in me through their word, that they may all be one, just as you, Father, are in me, and I in you, that they also may be in us, so that the world may believe that you have sent me. The glory that you have given me I have given to them, that they may be one even as we are one, I in them and you in me, that they may become perfectly one, so that the world may know that you sent me and loved them even as you loved me. Father, I desire that they also, whom you have given me, may be with me where I am, to see my glory that you have given me because you loved me before the foundation of the world. O righteous Father, even though the world does not know you, I know you, and these know that you have sent me.'"

John 17:1-25

7. Like Father Like Son

Think About It:

What does it mean to you that Jesus would pray and ask Father to give us the same glory they have always shared?

_____
_____
_____
_____
_____
_____
_____

Read Ephesians 5:1 and write out your thoughts.

_____
_____
_____
_____
_____
_____
_____
_____
_____
_____
_____
_____
_____
_____
_____
_____

8. Steps To Overcoming An Orphan Mentality

I want to discuss several steps that I believe are important to overcoming the orphan mentality in our lives, but the very first step is to admit that you struggle with it. I don't really know why we all seem to have such a hard time admitting that we struggle with an orphan mentality except that it is because we struggle with an orphan mentality. Let that sink it for a moment.

When you finally admit that there are areas in your heart that may need healing or simply areas where you need to grow up, then you can begin the process of doing so. To live in denial is to never experience healing and growth, but when you humble yourselves and admit that you need help, grace will flood you and teach you. God desires that we come to an understanding of our sonship, so if we cry out to Him, He will answer and Holy Spirit will help us.

As with anything in the Kingdom, repentance is the key to changing, but please don't mistake repentance with something you may have seen in church that resembles weeping and gnashing of teeth in some type of grief or sorrow. That is simply weeping and gnashing your teeth in grief and sorrow and most likely not truly a part of repentance. I am not saying it can't be or that when you see your brokenness that it will not cause you to weep. However, I feel that some people think that weeping over their brokenness is repentance and it is not. Repentance is changing the way you think and thereby changing what you are doing. True repentance brings you into freedom, not condemnation. True repentance causes you to step more fully into who you are

8. Steps To Overcoming An Orphan Mentality

in Christ, as you turn away and reject anything that exalts itself above the knowledge of who He is and who you are in Him!

Trust issues are a big deal with orphans, so we must overcome the tendencies we have to not trust people when we have given place to an orphan mentality in our lives. I know it may be hard to trust people when you have been hurt and betrayed by them, but you must learn to at least trust God. That is the starting point of having your ability to trust others restored. Remember, if you don't start somewhere, you will never get anywhere. Trust issues are so much a part of the make up of orphans because many feel that they have never had anyone they could trust.

The hymn writer said, *"I'm so glad I learned to trust Him, Precious Jesus, Savior, Friend!"* This line from the hymn, *'Tis So Sweet*, by Louisa M. R. Stead, says it perfectly. We must learn to trust Jesus and we must learn to trust in our Father God. He has never failed you, nor has He ever meant harm for you. Every good and perfect gift in your life has come from your Father, the Father of Lights, who loves you with an everlasting love. He is worthy of our praise and He is worthy of our trust.

I recently asked Father how I learned to trust Him. I am sure that I had trust issues when I first came to Him but as I got to know Him, they melted away. I wanted to understand when it was that I learned to trust Him. It isn't an easily answered question or really as simple as I had hoped it would be. The best way to articulate it is that it happened one encounter at a time, one step at a time, and sometimes, even one fall at a time. It was through all the issues, the great victories and the almost unbearable failures that I learned to trust God. It was in the midst of the struggles, when I expected judgement and anger from Him, but He only poured out grace and mercy on me, that my hard heart melted. He melted me with His love! Again and again He proved His love to me.

I look back at the songs that we sang through all those years and I see how the cry of my heart was to know Him and to see Him as He truly is. I wanted to know Him as my Father. I wanted to know the power that raised Christ from the dead that was now living in me. I cried out to know Him more, but my sinfulness always tried to keep me from Him. Much as Adam and Eve hid when they sinned in the garden, I would often want to hide in many things, including my prideful service of Him. However, at a very young age I had heard Father speak to me and instruct me clearly that no matter what happened, I should never run from Him but always run to Him. And that is precisely what I did. No matter how bad the situation, the failure, the sin, or whatever happened, I ran to Father! I found Him always faithful and I found Him always loving. I know many times I expected judgement, but I found only love. Correction? Yes, I found that! But never in a hateful or harsh way. He always poured out His love on me and even in the midst of discipline, He was so full of love that it melted my fear. Perfect love cast out fear! I found this to be so very true. Father's love is perfect. He has proven His love to me over and over again.

Next, I had to learn to be ok with who Father created me to be. This is much harder to do than it is to say. I often have heard people protest that no one is going to tell them who to be or how to act, all while wearing the fashion that someone else has influenced them to wear and using language that causes them to fit in with the modern vernacular. The list goes on and on.

We really are not as independent as we like to think. I see so many people trying to be someone else, but the truth is until you stop trying to be someone else, you can never truly be you! You were created to be unique and should not try to fit in with the crowd. You should simply be who God created you to be.

Until you stop trying to be someone else, you can never truly be you!

One of the most unique people I have ever known was our adopted daughter Leah, who came into our lives when she was 13. We did not really adopt her, she adopted us as her family. She was our first kid, before we had kids and boy did she give us an education on raising children. She had her own way of doing everything. I remember once remarking about the way she was dressed. It just didn't fit in with the way everyone else was dressing at the time and I was shocked at her reply. She basically told me that anyone can follow trends, but it takes someone special to start them. That girl was something else. She seemed to have no need to fit in or be be accepted by other people's opinion or approval. She is with the Lord now, after a long battle with cancer. She remained true to being who she was until her last moment here. I remember her saying to me one day before she passed, that she was not afraid at all to die, she was more afraid not to live! What a powerful statement.

Being ruled by what other people think about you will paralyze and keep you from experiencing the life God has for you. There is so much to accomplish, so many dreams to fulfill and so much to experience in our Father's Kingdom! We cannot let fear hold us back. Again, our fear should not be dying, our fear, so to speak, should be not ever living! Jesus came so that we could live an abundant life.

I wrote a song a few years ago, *I Am At Rest*, that addresses two of the issues which are steps to overcoming the orphan mentality. It is recorded on VC2's first worship CD entitled, Hope Is Here, and part of the lyrics simply state how I feel about my life. It really is a lifelong written song and if

8. Steps To Overcoming An Orphan Mentality

you truly knew my journey, you would know how powerful the statement is. The following is just part of the song:

I am at rest in Your righteousness,
I am at peace with who I am,
All of my shame has been wiped away,
I am made new, made new in You!

It took me a long time to be able to say those lines and mean it. Finding rest in His righteousness is essential to growing up as a son of God. Learning to be at peace with who I am and learning to be who Father created me to be has been a long journey. I am so glad I am able to know that He has removed all my guilt, all my shame and that in Him, I am made new!

You will not find peace with who you are until you become ok with who God made you to be. He created you to be you! He didn't make you to act like someone else. This is so important. If we are not careful, we can get pressed into a mold to become something that is acceptable to society or to the current fads. This is directly against the warnings of Paul to not be conformed to this world but to be transformed by the renewing of our minds. To what are we to renew our minds? We renew our minds to what God says about us! Our minds must be renewed to His pattern of us and what He calls us to be and who He has created us to be.

"I appeal to you therefore, brothers, by the mercies of God, to present your bodies as a living sacrifice, holy and acceptable to God, which is your spiritual worship. Do not be conformed to this world, but be transformed by the renewal of your mind, that by testing you may discern what is the will of God, what is good and acceptable and perfect."
Romans 12:1-2

To conform is to be pressed into a mold that you do not

fit in. It is to try to be something you are not or to try to fit somewhere you do not fit. God has called you to be you and the world needs to know the you He created. When you learn to do this, you will learn to rest in Him.

Learning to rest in who you are in Christ and who He is in you is a very integral part of overcoming an orphan mentality. Too many people strive to become righteous by their actions and fail to realize we have been made righteous by what Christ did on the cross and not by anything we do, except to believe in Him. The Bible tells us clearly that Christ did for us what we could not do for ourselves. He made us righteous. He was not sinful, yet He became sin for us so that we could become righteous like Him.

"For our sake he made him to be sin who knew no sin, so that in him we might become the righteousness of God."
2 Corinthians 5:21

God did this for our sake and by causing Jesus Christ to become sin for us, He opened the way for us to become His righteousness! The sooner you can accept this and stop quoting some Old Testament words like "There is none righteous, no not one" to make excuses for why you are not walking in all that you have been called to, then the sooner you can get to a place of rest in your Father. He has done for us what we could not do for ourselves. He has done for us what the law could not do, because it was weakened by our participation in it. He has made us righteous and because this is so, we can learn to rest in His righteousness.

Again, this is so key in overcoming the orphan nature because orphans often feel they have to work really hard to earn everything. This mentality short circuits Kingdom reality. We are not righteous because we do all the right things. It doesn't work that way. Righteousness is not right doing, but rather it is right standing. In Christ, we have been brought

8. Steps To Overcoming An Orphan Mentality

into right standing with the Father, not by our doings, but by what Jesus did for us. In fact, until you understand righteousness by faith, apart from the law, you can't even begin to do the right things. You will always strive in vain if your righteousness is based on your works. Orphan nature makes us feel that we must earn our keep, but a heart at rest in righteousness knows that the Keeper of Heaven and Earth has bought us with a precious price and we now belong to Him.

Learning to rest in His presence may be the hardest spiritual endeavor I have ever undertaken. I know how to work hard for the Lord as a good little servant. I did that for years. I know how to serve faithful in the house of the Lord and how to give myself and my time for others. I do not mean to diminish at all the need to serve faithfully. However, I do think that serving from a place of rest is MUCH BETTER than serving from a place of exhaustion. We must learn to rest in the Lord and to let everything we do flow out of that rest and intimacy with Him. This was my heart when I wrote the words, " I am at rest in Your righteousness. " It was only in His righteousness that I found my rest. Now I am able to work from a place of rest.

Another hard lesson for me to learn was that rest didn't mean not working, but it meant keeping my heart in a position to hear from Holy Spirit and to know what He was requiring of me, not what people required of me. Jesus indicated that He could only do what He saw His Father do and only say what He heard His Father say. This is a perfect picture of a place of rest in our Father. You see, rest is not the absence of work, it is the absence of striving!

Rest is not the absence of work, it is the absence of striving!

I find it very interesting that one of the only things we

8. Steps To Overcoming An Orphan Mentality

are told to strive to do in the entire counsel of God's Word is to rest. Strive to rest? Sounds like an oxymoron but I by no means think it is. If you are going to work at any spiritual endeavor, work to find that place of rest in the Father so that out of that place of knowing who you are in Him, you can do all that He has purposed for you to do.

"For if Joshua had given them rest, God would not have spoken of another day later on. So then, there remains a Sabbath rest for the people of God, for whoever has entered God's rest has also rested from his works as God did from his. Let us therefore strive to enter that rest, so that no one may fall by the same sort of disobedience."
Hebrews 4:8-11

Strive to enter the rest sounds a lot like work to us. It is really hard for us to see the word strive and not have negative connotations attached to it. It is not negative here at all but rather is a very positive thing. The Greek word translated strive here merely means hasten to do it, or be eager to do it. It means to move speedily by showing full diligence. We should show full diligence in learning to rest in the finished work of the cross and find ourselves in Christ having a righteousness that only comes by faith. It is ours in Christ! I think once you find it, and experience the peace and joy of resting in who you really are, you will find that when you stray from it, you eagerly want to get right back into that place of rest.

Holy Spirit longs to move us on into all the things that Father has for us. He longs for us to grow up into Christ and in this precious salvation into which we have been brought. As we learn to live and move and have our being in Him, we will find new and deeper places in the heart of our Father. In doing this, we find the Lord's Prayer answered as we see His Kingdom coming and His will being done, in and through us. It is in that place that we understand that we are indeed

8. Steps To Overcoming An Orphan Mentality

a chosen generation, a holy nation, a peculiar people, who have been called to manifest His glory here on the earth. We begin to shine brightly with the light that He filled us with when He called us out of darkness. We begin to rise as the sons of God throughout the earth, preparing the Kingdom for the arrival of our King—the One whom our hearts love and long for!

Think About It:

Do you feel you have come to the place of simply trying to be yourself? This is not an easy question to answer, but if you can be honest with yourself it wil help you address the areas Holy Spirit is wanting to help you grow up in.

Further Study:
Read Ephesians 2:11-22 to better understand peace.

9. Sonship and Sin

I believe many people in the church allow sin to keep them from walking in their sonship rights. I often found in my life that my shame of not getting things right, or my guilt over continued struggles kept me from walking in my authority. I allowed the enemy to convince me that I had no rights and I felt I was bound more to sin than to a Savior. I know I focused much of my prayer time, my thought life and my personal time with the Lord, on sin.

I began to seek the Lord at one point, knowing that I had to be missing something. As I studied the Word concerning sin, I kept seeing scriptures that pointed me toward the thought that Jesus had defeated sin on my behalf and I awoke to the fact that I was missing something. It was a revelation of the grace of God that woke me up to understand that Christ defeated sin and had set me free and that by His grace, was teaching me to live free even in the midst of darkness!

I want to look at how I have come to understand some of the points concerning sin and sonship and moreover, how sin affects us. It has helped me to understand these things. We will start by looking at someone who gave up his rights just because he was hungry, but more disconcerting is that he despised his place of sonship and laid down his authority.

"Once when Jacob was cooking stew, Esau came in from the field, and he was exhausted. And Esau said to Jacob, "Let me eat some of that red stew, for I am exhausted!" Therefore his name was called Edom. Jacob said, "Sell me your

9. Sonship and Sin

birthright now." Esau said, "I am about to die; of what use is a birthright to me?" Jacob said, "Swear to me now." So he swore to him and sold his birthright to Jacob. Then Jacob gave Esau bread and lentil stew, and he ate and drank and rose and went his way. Thus Esau despised his birthright."

Genesis 25:29-34

I want us to look closely at what Esau gave up this day and why he did it. He didn't give up his sonship. He didn't become an orphan that day. He didn't give up his inheritance. What Esau gave up this day was his authority. He gave up his rights as the first born. He gave up his seat and the authority that belongs to the first born or his birthrights.

His birthright meant:
- He would be the ruling member of the family or tribe, with judicial authority.
- He would receive a double portion of the family inheritance.
- He would become the priest or spiritual ruler of the family.
- There would always be special favor on him.

What did he give all of this up for? Momentary pleasure! It was his own desire to have something he wanted. He wasn't really about to die; but he thought his desires were about to kill him. This is what gets most of us. It feels like we are going to die if we don't get that thing that we want and we allow our fleshly desires to dictate what we will do. We lay down our authority to rule and reign over the situation, in exchange for the fulfillment of our desires, and we forfeit what is rightfully ours.

We do not lose our sonship when we sin, but we do lay aside our authority. At the place we deny our right to rule and reign, we decide to allow something to rule and reign over us. I believe this is a very important point for us. Reign, or be reigned over!

There is a difference in access and authority. The enemy does not have authority in our lives, he is always a thief, but we give him access by our disobedience. When we give the enemy access, he comes in like a thief and steals, kills, and destroys. That is all he knows how to do. We have been given authority over the enemy and must walk in it!

We cannot walk in the authority of God whilst surrendering to the enemy of our souls. We don't lose our sonship, but when we devalue it or despise it, we are refusing to walk in the authority that is rightfully ours. We choose the momentary over the lasting. This is part of the manifestation of the orphan mentality as well. The orphan nature always looks for a quick fix. A son holds on to who he is and produces long term fulfillment.

Esau devalued his birthright, his place of authority, by not embracing it. He did not see the value in it or see it worth anything. He placed his own personal needs above the place of authority that was given to him. Please don't think that this is only Old Covenant stuff. Let's take a look at a scripture in the New Testament that will explain more of this to us.

"See to it that no one fails to obtain the grace of God; that no "root of bitterness" springs up and causes trouble, and by it many become defiled; that no one is sexually immoral or unholy like Esau, who sold his birthright for a single meal. For you know that afterward, when he desired to inherit the blessing, he was rejected, for he found no chance to repent, though he sought it with tears."

Hebrews 12:15-17

Most translations call Esau immoral and godless. His tears, his begging, didn't change anything. He was lead by his fleshly desires and sought his own pleasure. Please notice that he didn't seek for grace to change, he only sought to have the blessing of his father. He did not really desire to be changed, just blessed!

Esau did not desire to be changed, just blessed!

Esau is much like the older son in the "Parable of the Running Father" found in Luke 15:11-24. Though he had the authority to do more than he had done, he laid it down or despised it and sought to serve his Father, seeking only to please him enough to gain access into what was already rightfully his. He did not understand his authority. He sought to please his father more than walk in his own authority.

We are sons of the Most High God and have been given authority to rule and reign over the things that once ruled and reigned over us. We have been called to have dominion and to be fruitful! In Christ, we have sonship, authority, and righteousness! We must not despise or demean the place that God has raised us up to. We must acknowledge the place of authority that God has called us into and understand it is not prideful to do so. I am by no means suggesting that we not live in a way that is pleasing to our Father, but I believe what pleases our Father God is that we walk in our authority!

"Let not sin therefore reign in your mortal body, to make you obey its passions. Do not present your members to sin as instruments for unrighteousness, but present yourselves to God as those who have been brought from death to life, and your members to God as instruments for righteousness. For sin will have no dominion over you, since you are not under law but under grace."

Romans 6:12-14

We have the right and the grace to walk free, but we must

make the choice. Grace empowers us to live the life that Jesus died for us to have. He has brought us out of sin and into sonship. I do believe sin has been dealt with at the cross, but I also believe we must learn to walk in this freedom we have been given. Grace does not overlook sin, but rather empowers us to overcome it and to live righteously!

Jesus brought us out of sin and into sonship!

Don't trade in your authority in Christ for a momentary fulfillment! We have Kingdom work to do. We have to learn to walk in our authority. We have been set free from sin so we are no longer slaves to it. We don't have to wait until we die to be set free from sin. Jesus has already done this for us. My friend Georgian Banov said this, *"If we are only set free from sin when we die, then Jesus isn't our Savior, death is."*

So how do I overcome sin? The truth is we already are free from sin in Christ, and now we have to grow in grace and learn to walk in our freedom. We cannot continue on in sin—that is not the purpose of grace. Instead, we must allow grace to teach us how to live upright and godly lives even in this present darkness.

"For the grace of God has appeared, bringing salvation for all people, training us to renounce ungodliness and worldly passions, and to live self-controlled, upright, and godly lives in the present age, waiting for our blessed hope, the appearing of the glory of our great God and Savior Jesus Christ, who gave himself for us to redeem us from all lawlessness and to purify for himself a people for his own possession who are zealous for good works."

Titus 2:11-14

Jesus came to reveal the Father to us and to show us how to live as sons. He lived as a faithful son, going about His Father's business, doing His Father's will, just as we are sup-

9. Sonship and Sin

posed to. He was our example of how it can be done. He is the example of us, revealing to us what it looks like for a human to be fully submitted to the Father's will. Remember that 1 John 3:1 declares that we have become sons of God.

"See what kind of love the Father has given to us, that we should be called children of God; and so we are. The reason why the world does not know us is that it did not know him."
1 John 3:1

The Greek word used for children is listed in the Strongs Concordance as *5043 téknon* – **properly, a child; (figuratively) anyone living in full dependence on the heavenly Father, i.e. fully (willingly) relying upon the Lord in glad submission.** This prompts God to transform them into His likeness. *A child living in willing dependence* illustrates how we must all live in utter dependence upon the Lord (moment-by-moment), drawing guidance (care, nurture) from our heavenly Father. 5043 (*téknon*) emphasizes the childlike (not childish) attitude of heart that willingly (gladly) submits to the Father's plan.

So we have died to sin and now we are alive to righteousness. We are called to live holy and righteous lives by the power of grace! In Christ we have the right and authority to do this.

"What shall we say then? Are we to continue in sin that grace may abound? By no means! How can we who died to sin still live in it? Do you not know that all of us who have been baptized into Christ Jesus were baptized into his death? We were buried therefore with him by baptism into death, in order that, just as Christ was raised from the dead by the glory of the Father, we too might walk in newness of life. For if we have been united with him in a death like his, we shall certainly be united with him in a resurrection like his. We know that our old self was crucified with him in order that

the body of sin might be brought to nothing, so that we would no longer be enslaved to sin. For one who has died has been set free from sin. Now if we have died with Christ, we believe that we will also live with him. We know that Christ, being raised from the dead, will never die again; death no longer has dominion over him. For the death he died he died to sin, once for all, but the life he lives he lives to God. So you also must consider yourselves dead to sin and alive to God in Christ Jesus."

Romans 6:1-11

As sons of God we have been set free from sin. We are now slaves to righteousness and not slaves to sin. As sons of God we have authority, we have rights and we have business to be about—our Father's business. We must give ourselves fully to the work of our Father.

Let the sons of God arise!

Think About It:

Do you believe that when you mess up God is unhappy with you? Why?

___

How do we overcome sin?

___

9. Sonship and Sin

Further Study:

Study Hebrews Chapters 8, 9 & 10 to gain a greater understanding of what Christ has done for us.

10. Stories Of Those Who Overcame

I shared some of the information from this book at a church where I was a guest speaker and after the message a nice older lady came to me and said she greatly identified with what I was sharing and basically gave me a huge "*Amen*" to what I had shared. I thought she was simply identifying what God had done in her through the message only to be awaken to the realization that she was saying much more. "*I was an orphan,*" she said. I don't remember my response exactly but obviously it was a preacher type one because she knew I did not get it. She repeat, "*I was actually orphaned at a young age so for many years now I have been on a journey with Father God as He was setting me free from the feelings of abandonment and all that went along with being orphaned as a child.*"

I found out that this precious lady was actually a guest that day and didn't attend that church. It blew my mind that God had brought someone to not only confirm the things I was saying and encourage me, but also to help her see how far she had come in her journey and to celebrate her freedom. I wish I would have had cognizance of mind to ask her to write down some of her story for this book. Alas, I didn't realize at that moment that it was a book. However, I have asked a few people I know who have been set free, or they are being set free, from an orphan mentality, to share their stories. I hope their point of view will resonate within you and help you see how important it is for us to be set free.

Christopher Daigle

There is not enough book space to completely explain

the journey that God has brought me through, or this book would be about 10 chapters longer. I do however hope to share a little of my journey to show how God has been setting me free from the orphan mentality.

Growing up, I always felt out of place. I always felt that I was the weird kid. I was different. I remember being on medication at a young age, wondering why no one else my age had to live this way. I was often made fun of for having to take medication, how I dressed, how I acted and was considered socially awkward. It was at the age of six that I began to desire to be someone else. I tried to be like everyone I thought was cool. It produced a life of me trying to impress everyone.

In all honesty, this book could be titled, "The Life of Christopher Daigle." I have identified so deeply with many of these behaviors. One of the statements Pastor Chad made got me. Basically he said often we try to appear more spiritual than we are, hoping that people will see what God is doing in our lives.

I remember the first day someone came up to me and said, *"I see the fire of God all over you, I see Jesus in you."* You might as well have told me I was a super model. I believe their motives were pure in encouraging me, but the orphan nature in me was so desperate for attention that I received the compliment like a drug. It got worse when I discovered the gifts of the Holy Spirit.

I remember the first day I spoke an accurate word of prophecy. It was a beautiful moment that I made a monument. It became a look at me, look at how God uses me, look what I can do mentality. I walked around intentionally trying to show off my gift. I did this because I felt rejected. I really wanted people to see how spiritual I was, hoping they would accept me. I also did this in an attempt to hide

10. Stories Of Those Who Overcame

my brokenness because I was ashamed of it. The truth is I discovered at an early stage that you can look spiritual and have no real relationship with Jesus. I felt like a fraud.

This lifestyle didn't cause too many issues until it started getting me promotions in the body of Christ. I'm thankful I knew that I wasn't ready for a pulpit, but that desire to be seen caused me an internal struggle. I began trying to bury these behaviors of brokenness and the desire for affirmation, pretending they weren't there, trying to make my motives pure. I don't care how hard I tried and strived, I knew it was still there. I wanted so badly to feel important.

I remember I had a sit down with a leader of a house of prayer in Manchester, NH, and she said to me straight, *"Christopher, I can tell you what your struggle is: you're dealing with the orphan mentality."*

To me that sounded like a cancer diagnosis. I identified that if I acted like an orphan, and people saw an orphan, I was no longer important. I began to want to kill off these symptoms, and thus began my life of striving. After a few months of trying really hard to be a son, I started leading worship. The leaders I had at the time were very aware of my struggle and were counseling me through it. They cared very much for me and were very instrumental in my journey in that season. They often said to me how they wished I knew how loved I was; not only by them, but by God as well. We worked through this together and I owe so much to them.

The issue was that our worship leader was leaving and we had no one to step up. I told God I was willing to step in, I just wanted to make sure I didn't act like an orphan. I struggled every week with the thought of having to die to myself, thinking that this was the way to freedom. It wasn't.

Often my prayer sounded something like, *"God, I lay my*

life down, I die to this desire to want to feel important. I make this about you, and I ask that I become invisible and content with who you have made me." Nothing changed, after each set I still wanted to hear "good job" or how anointed I was. I hid in false humility saying, *"It was the Lord."* Someone once said to me, *"Well it was good, but it wasn't that good."* It was hard for me to just say thank you since I knew in my heart I was fishing for a compliment.

The thing is, wanting to feel important is a normal trait for a human being. The truth was, I just wanted to know that I was important in the Lord's eyes. God didn't want me to become invisible and what I was really asking was for help to find my sense of importance in Him, not in the worship set. My heart's cry was always, *"Please help me see that I matter."* This doesn't happen by killing off symptoms. I needed to understand sonship apart from the works of the flesh.

I wanted to matter in my own eyes. I have always wanted to be pleasing to everyone I met, especially my earthly father. When I got saved in January of 2014, this attempt to please everyone became a part of my relationship with the Lord. I just wanted God to be proud of me, thinking that He was only proud when I got things right. I lived this whole walk with the Lord trying to do everything right. I felt a sense of significance if I made sacrifices. I thought Abraham, in Genesis, had special favor with God because he was willing to give up his son. I thought the more I sacrificed, the better God saw me and the more proud He was of me. I was mistaken.

When I learned you could hear God's voice and respond, my life became an adventure. I took delight in hearing His voice. If God asked me to do something, I would do it thinking that since I passed the test, I earned something that made me different than the person next to me. If you haven't figured it out by now, let me help you see that I really

10. Stories Of Those Who Overcame

struggled with pride. One morning, I had one of those moments: a chance to please God —insert sarcasm here.

I woke up on September 18th, 2016, and heard Holy Spirit say, *"I want you to go to Hilltop Church."* In all honesty my first response was "why?" I love HIlltop Church. It's an amazing church in Cambridge, MA, that I had visited on many occasions. I really didn't want to go because I wanted to rest before I had to lead worship that evening at my home church. On top of that it was an hour away, and I had to drive through Boston traffic to get there. It was an inconvenience to say the least, but Holy Spirit won the arguement and I went.

I had no idea what to expect other than the fact that I loved the Worship, and the Word spoken was always convicting. What I didn't know was that Chad Waller, whom I had never met, was a guest speaker, and this was a Holy Spirit set up. Chad preached on being a son, and identified what a spiritual orphan can look like. I listened in awe and tears, realizing I was still living as an orphan and didn't know how deep this mentality went, or how much it was affecting everything I did.

As I sat there listening, I knew this message was for me. I had been living this life, trying to please a Father who was already pleased with me. I believed every time I failed, He was mad at me. I believed that my salvation and righteousness was all on me to get it right. I thought every time I got it wrong, I was a less than.

At the end of the sermon I went up for altar ministry. I received a few prophetic words that confirmed some things, but to be honest I wasn't paying attention. I felt in my heart that I had to hug this man and thank him. I didn't realize what impact that would have on both our lives. He gave me his number and told me if I needed anything, to call him. He didn't realize I wasn't apart of this church but was just

10. Stories Of Those Who Overcame

a visitor. God does incredible things to reach His children.

Six months later, I type this story while in Georgia. I am now an intern at VC2, and have the pleasure of learning from this family of God under the authority of Pastors Chad and Melinda Waller. The Lord has been doing such a big work in my heart and I am so blessed to walk into deeper revelations of sonship through this journey.

Since I've been in Georgia, I've been experiencing a lot of freedom. My favorite part about being here is I get to do life with Chad and Melinda and the people of VC2. One of my favorite things about Pastor Chad is the fact that he's so open and transparent about where he's at with the Lord. My favorite times with him are when he tells me when God is convicting his character. This has been huge for me because I grew up thinking every time I was corrected, it was because I was a failure. In all honesty, anytime I received correction from a leader, I wanted to run. I didn't want people to see what I struggled with. This was a big part of the orphan mentality for me. I also didn't take into account that fathers correct their sons because they love them. When I was a kid, I hated being corrected by my father. I felt like a failure and that I had to fix myself so he wouldn't be disappointed in me. The truth was, my father wasn't disappointed with me, he just wanted to see me succeed. I'm now realizing what this scripture means:

"...It's the child he loves that he disciplines; the child he embraces, he also corrects. God is educating you; that's why you must never drop out. He's treating you as dear children. This trouble you're in isn't punishment; it's training, the normal experience of children. Only irresponsible parents leave children to fend for themselves..."
Hebrews 12:6-8 MSG

For the first time of my life, I enjoy saying yes to God,

even if that requires me to say no to a great opportunity. Some of the ways I have overcome orphan behaviors is by saying no to things my flesh once really wanted. Usually, the things I had to say no to were the things I wanted. It's amazing really. I have been trying my whole life to feel important and giving someone like that a mic can be dangerous. I wonder how hard it is for a leader to not give someone a mic in a church service because they have, what they believe, is a word from the Lord. Even though someone appears to be passionate and bold, you can tell when they just want the mic to be heard.

I now understand all the times I was told no. Often the word I had on my heart was spoken through someone else. At the beginning, I hated this. Just the other day this happened here at VC2. I had a word that was nagging my heart. I whispered it to Chad and he acknowledged it, and not two minutes later, the woman leading the song on the worship team gave the same word. God was showing me that He loves to move through me, but He doesn't need me. What I mean is, others are capable as well. He still sobers me and reminds me daily with little things like this.

When I was struggling with the orphan mentality, I was jealous when I didn't get to share the word on my heart. I would feel impulsive in my heart because I wanted to share my thought before anyone else said it so that it appeared I heard from heaven first. Or worse, I would say things after someone shared a revelation like, "Oh, God was speaking that to me too," or "I was getting that same thing." This caused words that were from God to be said at the wrong time or in the wrong place. It was all about me. When I didn't get the credit, I said to myself, "No one saw that the word came from me. No one saw my prophetic gift!" But now, as a son, I rejoice that I heard my Father, and am excited to see that my sister in Christ did as well. The gifts are to be used to edify and strengthen the one receiving the word, not puff me up in my spiritual identity.

My desire to feel important, to feel wanted, and to feel like I needed to impress people starting dying as I began to realize that my Father loved me. The most amazing thing that I have discovered about my Father in heaven is that He corrects, disciplines, challenges, and encourages me into change. When I realized that correction was part of love, I realized my earthly father, Mark, is an amazing man who loves me very much. When I realized my father has always loved me, I no longer felt like an orphan. It has been so amazing to see what God has done in my heart. My perspective of my life has changed and I no longer feel like a victim. The truth is I never was, but I felt like one and believed I was. Today, in my heart I truly feel accepted by God, and this gives me rest to know I am no longer bound by being concerned if everyone else accepts me. To know He is pleased with me makes all the difference! Now that I know I'm not a victim, I can live as a son, and this journey will be of me learning what that means and walking it out.

John Morgan Bolt

In 2012 a friend of mine told me about this church that had really loud worship, and thought I might like it. The next Sunday, I walk into the cafe area of VC2 and there was no one to be found. As I stopped to look around, the love of God washed over me and this phrase slipped out of my mouth: *"I'm home."* I slipped into the sanctuary, found a place up front, and did my best to hide there. As the worship began, I had already decided in my mind that I was going to worship with everything I had.

Throughout my past, I had been to many churches; some with friends, some with family, and almost always I could feel the religious tension in the air as I began to pour out my heart in full abandon to God. Not knowing the culture, I'd simply made my mind up to give God everything I had.

10. Stories Of Those Who Overcame

I thought to myself, *"These people don't know me. I don't care what they think. If they don't like it, oh well."* At the time, all I had to give God was the hurt and the pain still fresh in my mind that had stemmed from years of disappointment, rejection, and the devastation of divorce. I had experienced divorce as a child with my parents, and then later, as a husband.

As the worship started that Sunday morning, with my eyes closed, I began to clap, jump, shout, laugh, and any other expression that came to mind to empty myself in front of my Savior. I wasn't worried about what was appropriate or what anyone else thought. I refused to slow down long enough to hear or feel any religious precepts that would tell me the way I worshiped was wrong. When the music was over, the same man who was worshipping next to me got up on stage and had the biggest smile on his face. He announced himself as the Pastor of the church, and took a moment to point me out. I had a feeling he would do this because I was used to people calling me out in churches. I began to prepare myself for some religious, hyper-prophetic nonsense. He instead used phrases like, *"We're going to be best friends. We love you."* And then he said, *"I feel like Jonathan and David whose hearts were knit together in friendship and in love."* I sat there and smiled, expecting this, saying to myself, "Big whoop..."

The problem was that I had no idea what it felt like to have a family. A loving family where fathers raised sons. My earthly father did all he knew to do, and to no fault of his own, did the best to show me Christ and to give us a strong foundation, but was still rendered ill equipped because of brokenness in his own life.

In the years to come, Pastor Chad and VC2 did something that no church family had ever been willing to do; they gave me room to be myself, no matter what that looked like at the moment. Through worship and mentoring, the issues of my soul began to come to the surface. One by one, God in his mercy began to heal and make whole many many places in my life. One of those issues was anger.

Without getting into too much detail, just know that rage, anger and hatred are well known to me and my family. They were great motivators in a pinch, and can get a lot done in a short amount of time, but the aftermath is always more painful than the progress. Growing up, anger was an emotion someone else made you feel and it was not your responsibility to control it until the anger was satisfied. Phrases like, "I'm angry! Now this is what you get," and, "I told you not to make me upset! Now I have to punish you for that," were the justifications for rule breaking in my mothers eyes. So when I read in **Ephesians 4:26** the phrase "**Be angry and sin not**," you could see how I had trouble understanding that.

With no one to teach me how to deal with anger, or any emotion for that matter, I just did what I had to in order to get through the moment. That meant taking it all in and holding the pain and hurt just to pour it out on others later on. Even though I was saved, filled with Holy Spirit, and worshiping with all abandon, the pain still was there. This is why I needed to be in a safe place for a long time. The great thing about being a Son of God is that nothing in the world scares you. Not even someone else's dysfunction or problems. Not because they exist and we just ignore them with some religious habit, but because you know how great your Father in heaven is. The more I learned about who I was as a son, the more Holy Spirit began to bring to the surface and deal with the things in my life that I had coped with and allowed room for in my life.

I would love to say one day it all just disappeared, but it was a process. Every chance I got to obey the Word, follow the pulling of Holy Spirit, or to serve those around me, I jumped at it no matter the cost. The good news is that I have learned through the years that my emotions are not good and evil, but are a gift from the Father. They can measure things that cannot be seen, but are not the ultimate truth in every situation. I was not a sinner (someone who knows right from wrong and chooses wrong) just because I was angry, but it's what I did under the inspiration of that emotion that determined my level of obedience to my Father. Now I can be angry and have learned to manage my decisions as well as my reactions because I have been given a spirit of power, love and self-control.

Jesus said one of the reasons He came to earth was to reveal the Father and if Christ is in me, than He is revealing the Father through my life. If I have a damaged or warped image of what a father is, then I won't be able to show the world the right version. I can then only show a perversion of who He really is. So I have made it my mission as a man, as a husband, and as a father myself now, to show the world who the best Father in all of existence is. If you want your life to have meaning and purpose, learn to be a son. Learn who you have become through salvation and then ask the hard questions: Who am I? Why am I alive? How can I learn more about You, Papa God?

Dani Way Lassiter

I spent the majority of my youth being a people pleaser and an acceptance addict. Being a Christian in public schools didn't cater well to that. I quickly took on social anxiety and as hard as I tried to be myself I found myself being a chameleon to fit in with those around me. If I was around church people, I would talk spiritual and have anxiety over trying to sound spiritual enough in my public spoken prayer or the angle my hands were raised with my pinkies just ever so lightly pointing outward. If I was at school around non believers or Sunday only Christians, I would passively laugh at things I knew were wrong or agree with things I didn't believe. I would act in ways a believer wouldn't and shouldn't act. I thought that just a little compromise was okay. Especially if it was mainly kept in the dark.

When attention and affection from men came into play in High School, it was a dangerous game changer that left me craving for more. This emptiness I was trying to fill was insatiable. I knew from church songs and Bible stories that God loved me and that He was supposed to be all I needed, but this love from guys was tangible and gave me instant gratification.

I was an orphan and didn't even know it. Like most broken people, I continued in cycles of bad decisions until I hit my rock bottom. For me, that didn't come until I went through a series of consequences caused by compromise and bad choices in friendships and love. In a matter of 7 years I experienced rape, abuse, unhealthy dating relationships, countless drunken nights to quiet my mind and numb the pain, a miscarriage, the plan B pill, another failed marriage, and a child born out of wedlock by another man during my divorce, and then another child conceived out of wedlock.

I thought God's plan for me was over. During these times I had never been so close to wanting to end my life. I had never felt like more of a failure or a mistake. I was so completely lost. It was then I realized I had a spiritual identity crisis. I didn't know who I was. I didn't understand or have revelation of what it really meant to be a child of God, for God to love me or for Jesus to wash my sins away. I realized I believed a lot of what I felt, or a lot of what the world told me about God and what He thought of me. I believed a lot of lies. It wasn't until countless heartbreaks that I realized men could not truly love me fully, faithfully, unconditionally or at my very darkest and worst. They could not fulfill my longings.

10. Stories Of Those Who Overcame

The only one who kept calling my name and pulling close was the very one I pushed away and put aside for short term satisfaction: my Father, and the lover of my soul, Jesus. When I got the real revelation of who He was to me and who I was to Him, I was so wrecked and it seemed irrevocably broken. My mind raced with questions like, *"How is this even possible? Why would you want me? What is the catch?"*

The catch was, I had to surrender. He wanted all of my love, all of my affection, all of my thoughts and my life. He wanted to be my one true love, my Father, my provider, my strength, my hope and peace.

The phrase *"Broken and bound heirs of God's kingdom,"* came to me one day. I know it sounds contradicting to what the Bible describes for the life of an heir with Christ. Besides that, what kind of royal heir (prince or princess) in any epic novel or movie would, by their own choice, live their life or rule their kingdom bound in chains in the dungeon of their castle? None!

The sad thing is, many sons and daughters of God do this and choose to try to live out their destinies from this place, most without much success. It doesn't matter how many songs you sing about freedom or verses you quote about grace, you won't ever fully understand or comprehend the meaning of either until you learn to fully submit to Father God. You have to receive and have revelation of your identity, release the weighted chains brought on by your sin because He already paid with His life to break those chains off of you. You have to drop the mask of shame you carry and hide behind in order to put on His glory and the armor of God. If you choose not to, you rob yourself of the fullness of His Joy. He is a God who takes what the world deems as insignificant and gives it purpose!

Your flesh and the enemy want to tell you that you're

10. Stories Of Those Who Overcame

never going to change, but once you surrender, God begins the process of changing old for new, giving you beauty for the ashes. When you accept Christ as your Savior, you die to your flesh (*Greek: Sarx strongs:4561: the flesh, denotes mere human nature, the earthly nature of man apart from divine influence, and therefore prone to sin and opposed to God*) and now the life you live is one through Christ Jesus. He adopted you in. You are a son or a daughter of the Creator, the one true God! The one who has the final say!

So when your dead and rotten flesh tries to rise up from the dead like *"Tales from the Crypt"* and speak lies to you, remind it who IS currently ALIVE in you! Remind it who you are and whose you are! If God is for you, who can be against you!?

Amanda Knowles

I didn't really know where to begin or if anyone would even want to know my testimony. In that alone, I realized how important it was for me to read Pastor Chad's book. However, I never would have imagined the process that would go along with reading it. I realized how much I struggle/struggled with the orphan mentality.

I think back over my life and can say there are lots of things that have slowly progressed to create this mentality. I didn't always feel this way. I remember a time in my life where I was extremely confident or at least I thought I was. So, I guess I will go back to the beginning.

When I was born, my mother was only 16. She lived at home with her parents. So, I went home with them from the hospital. However, my mother didn't end up keeping me. Her parents kept me and by the time I was about a year and a half they adopted me. Unfortunately, my grandfather passed away 2 months after they adopted me. My grandmother was raising me by herself until she remarried when I was about

10. Stories Of Those Who Overcame

3 years old.

I didn't really realize that anything was different about my life from any of the other kids around. I had 2 parents (grandparents) who were raising me, providing for me, and loved me. I also had a momma who I would see whenever she was visited or whenever she happened to live close enough for me to see her. I didn't realize that there was anything different. I guess as I got a little older and was in school for a few years, I realized I didn't know who my father was. I didn't even know his name. I asked my grandmother one time and to be honest now I don't even remember what she told me. However, I do remember she didn't tell me who he was and that the greatest impact was I realized it looked like it hurt her that I was asking. I didn't ever want to do anything to hurt my grandmother. The love that I had for her, I don't think I have ever loved anyone the way I loved her.

At this point, I always wondered why my father wasn't involved in my life or why I didn't know who he was, but it didn't really affect me at the point in my life. When I was 14 years old two weeks before my 15th birthday, my grandmother passed away. I felt like my world ended. I felt lost. It left me with my step-grandfather. My momma tried to get me to come live with her at this point, but I was old enough to know that the only reason she really wanted me to live with her was because I got a check from when my real grandfather passed away. I knew even then my mother had an issue with drugs and that was her priority in her life.

My curiosity of who my father was grew at this point, I approached my mom and asked who he was. On my 16th birthday, I received a birthday card from my mom with a letter enclosed. Inside the letter, she proceeded to tell me "Oh yeah by the way, your dad's name is and you have brothers too". I didn't wait for her to come or call to tell me more. I had a very good friend who helped me find him. To finally know who he was very exciting, but scary at the same time.

I thought my quest at knowing my dad and having him in my life was going to be great. However, I was young and didn't take into account that I had grown up without him in my life and things weren't necessarily going to just go perfectly together because he was my dad. Our relationship struggled because of things that happened in his life that I didn't understand. At this point, I felt like yet again I was completely alone. I had lost my grandmother, my step-grandfather had remarried and I was just in the way, my momma only wanted me because of the money she could get, and my dad was a stranger that I didn't know how to build a relationship.

I found myself alone. So at 16, I was going to rent my own place to live. However, I ended up living with my great grandfather or staying at a friend's house until the end of my junior year in high school. The summer between my junior and senior year, I went to stay at my mom's to help her with my brother and sister who were 5. She had surgery and needed help for a few weeks.

I ended up meeting a guy and started dating him. In just a few weeks of knowing him, we got engaged. You couldn't tell me anything. I thought I knew best. However, at the end of summer I came back home to my dads to get ready for my senior year in high school. I was excited to start my senior year and to share that I had gotten engaged. My happiness didn't last very long. My dad and step-mom did not approve of the guy I was engaged to. I made it through until Christmas break. When I mentioned wanting to go to see my boyfriend for the holidays, my step-mom said no. This lead to quite a bit of disagreement and ended in my being stubborn or you could just say stupid. One day when my dad and step-mom were at work, I packed all my things and left. I moved in with my boyfriend and caused quite a bit of hurt and anger.

While living with my boyfriend, I ended up not going back to school. I quit half way through my senior year. Also the man I thought was who I would marry, ended up being what I would say in the past as a mistake became a great life lesson. In this situation, I know this is one of the most memorable events that God put someone in my life. I met a young lady and her parents. They were great Christian people and showed God's love. They opened the home and hearts to me. I started going to church with them and began seeing people who had a true relationship with God.

I could continue to share lost more things that have happened in my life. The main thing I have realized is that what I thought about myself and how I thought others saw me was something that happened over night. I was many years of feeling like people were always leaving me or telling me that because of the mistakes I made that I was never going to do anything worthwhile in my life. Praise God! I know that even though I struggle with those thoughts, God loves me with a love like no one else ever will. It doesn't matter the mistakes I have made or what others think of me. He has placed an amazing church family in my life that are supportive and walk through life with me in love.

I have seen God work in so many ways in my life in just the 2 years. Through losing my job, having to move from the home we had lived in for 4 years, my husband having 2 back surgeries and losing his job, God has shown me that if we are faithful and trust in him in all things He will provide for us even when we don't see a way. There were times we didn't know how we were going to pay bills, but He has always provided. He is a good Father!

10. Stories Of Those Who Overcame

Think About It:

What would be your story of overcoming the orphan mentality? Consider writing it out here.

_____
_____
_____
_____
_____
_____
_____
_____
_____
_____
_____
_____
_____
_____

11. No More Spiritual Orphans

I believe we can make a huge impact in the generations if we address the issue of spiritual orphans and become determine to raise up sons who know their Father. I don't believe it is enough that we just sing of a good, good Father, though that is a great start, but we must also teach our sons and daughters about this good Father and teach them how to trust Him. I believe that fathers must awaken to their responsibility and their role in this venture of knowing Father God. As earthly fathers, we are called to be reflections of our Heavenly Father, as I pointed out in Chapter Seven. We are to represent our Father to this world just as Jesus did.

There is a statement that I often make to our home church and every time I make it, I feel the weight of it. Often when I have said it, I have felt as if it is too hard a saying and have at times felt I should not say it. Let me be quick to add, I don't feel conviction of Holy Spirit not to say it, but I hear the hordes of darkness screaming at me to not say such. If that makes you uncomfortable, so be it, but that is how it feels.

The statement is simply this: ***If we don't like the condition of our city we have no one to blame but ourselves. We are the ones who were called to make a difference here and if there is no difference in this city and if things aren't changing, it is on us! We are called to extend the Kingdom of Heaven on this earth. We are called to do the things Jesus did, and more!***

You may disagree; no worries if you do, but I can't get

11. No More Spiritual Orphans

away from the biblical mandate for the church to go, to be salt, be light and release the glory of God in the earth. While we sit around praying for revival, I fear God sits enthroned in heaven awaiting the day we awake to realize we are the revival for which we are praying. His glory, that He has invested in us, is revival. The hope of glory lives in us. The hope that the world will see revival resides inside of us! Jesus is **EVER INTERCEDING** for us. For what, then, am I waiting? We already have the mandate to go. Yes, pray, and then go!

Don't wait for some prophesied coming revival, when the hearts of fathers will be turned to the children. You want to see that revival happen? Then turn your heart toward your children, begin pouring into them spiritually and helping them grow up in their call and purpose. Don't just focus on you getting over your stuff, help them not get into the stuff that trapped you! Begin crying out for the next generation. Yes, pray, but then go and do something to help them. Get involved with training the next generation. Let's put an end to a generation of spiritual orphans. Get involved with rescuing lives! If every kid had an adult that they felt truly cared about them and was in their corner fighting for them, the world would be a different place. We cannot just talk about the decline of this generation, pinning names on them meant to demean them, but we must get involved in helping them find what God has purposed them to be. Again, if we don't like where things are headed, what will we do about it? I so desire that parents would give as much care to their kids spiritual training as they do to their earthly education.

I know we can make a difference. I see it happening. We are seeing a generation rise up who know Father God as a good Father and it is giving them confidence to fearlessly do the things they are called to do. They are drinking deeply of Father's love and His perfect love is casting out fear and giving them boldness. It is incredible to watch this young

11. No More Spiritual Orphans

generation as they follow the leading of the Lord.

I remember one day a man mentioned to me that his knee was hurting and that he possibly would have to have surgery. There was a suggestion made that we pray for his knee, so we began to pray for him. One of my daughters, who was only 12 or so at the time, began to pray very aggressively, whereas I was praying very calmly, and was praying a nice little prayer. I started to quieten my daughter down to pray in a manner that I felt the man could receive better and one that, in my mind, was more fitting for the situation. Just as I thought to do that, I heard so clearly inside of me, *"Oh, you want to make her as ashamed of me as you are?"*

I was floored, shocked, maybe even a little offended. I knew I would have to argue that one out with Holy Spirit later, but for the moment I conceded. It was sometime later that I heard a report from this man that his knee was healed that day. He stated that he had never heard a little girl pray quite like that girl did, but whatever she did, it sure did make his knee feel better.

I will never forget the feeling I had that day. I wasn't a novice at this and it certainly wasn't my first rodeo. How could Holy Spirit think that I was ashamed of Him? Or why would he even say that to me? It really is very simple. I didn't want Him to make me look bad. At the time, still struggling with an orphan mentality, I wanted to be respected, liked, and I needed to fit in. I did not want to be rejected or put down. I wanted to do the right thing! Yet, truly the right thing was to pray for this man and release the power of God into Him! It wasn't about me, it was about what God wanted to do for this man.

Now, before you judge me, let me tell you that I didn't even realize that was there. If you had told me any of this I would have denied it. It is not until you are confronted with

11. No More Spiritual Orphans

the situation, and Holy Spirit brings revelation, that you can repent and move on. I thought I had dealt with all of that junk and was walking in freedom. Maybe I was, but there was more freedom that Father wanted to bring me into. He wanted to set me free from caring about what men thought of me. He wanted to set me free from myself! I am so thankful that He exposed it and gave me grace to deal with it.

It is interesting to note that I felt Holy Spirit speak to me the day that my daughter did this, showing me that she did not know to be afraid of someone's opinion of her faith because I had never taught her to be. In fact, we had raised our kids to be fearless with their faith and to go after God with all their hearts. She didn't know to pray any differently in public than we did at home. She was only doing what she had seen modeled. Wow! This floored me. I was the one saying one thing, but fear had me doing another. I am so thankful that the daughter I had raised in the faith taught me a lesson that day.

Story after story could be told about how our kids have encouraged us in the faith and how glorious it is to watch them serve the Lord. When I hear people talking about how bad this generation is I simply think, "You should meet my kids!" Our church is full of young people who are in love with the King and are serving Him faithfully. I preach at other churches and often see tons of young people who are faithful in the Kingdom of God. Open your eyes and you will see that not only are the fields ripe unto harvest, but they are filling with faithful laborers ready to take the harvest!

I am overwhelmed many times when I look up at our worship team and see so many young people leading, several are my own kids, others are young people that we have poured our lives into for years. I look around at the outreaches we do throughout the city and see kids serving, and my heart swells. Please don't waste your words on me telling me that this generation doesn't want anything to do with God or with church or whatever. They do! They simply need a real experience with a real God, and when they taste His real love, they will surrender to it and serve with all their hearts. We have seen it over and over again.

I am completely blown away by how fast this generation is getting revelation about things it took me much longer to comprehend. They are growing in the ways of the Lord and so much fruit can be seen in their lives. I watch some of the younger ones teach with such great authority, something that once was seen to be for the older, more mature saints. Sometimes my kids share things that God has spoken to them through His Word and I am just amazed at the depth. There is such a divine acceleration that is taking place in the body of Christ as folks who are coming into the Kingdom of God, are growing up at a much faster pace than they seemed to have in the past generations. Maybe this is just how it feels to me, and maybe it isn't really so. Or maybe I was just a slow learner. Either way, I am just glad I finally got it and I am excited to see all that God is doing in a generation that is seeking His face!

Melinda and I are now focused on our grandchildren, pouring into them and releasing to them the love that we have found in Father. We are washing their futures with our prayers. We are praying into their destinies and thanking God that they will go further, see more and accomplish things we only dreamed of! We will do everything we can to wipe out the orphan mentality and the feelings of hopelessness that have plagued the church for many years. We are the hopeful– **the hope filled!**

We are filled with hope that sons are awakening to who they were created to be!

Jesus said He would not leave us as orphans, and He did

11. No More Spiritual Orphans

not. He sent His precious Holy Spirit, the Spirit of Adoption to adopt us into the family. We cannot just rejoice in this truth for ourselves, but must make sure we bring the next generation into this revelation and help them to grow up into this thought much sooner than we did.

Think About It:

The revival the world is waiting for lives inside of you. Write down your thoughts on this statement.

_____
_____
_____
_____
_____
_____
_____
_____
_____

Further Study:

Read 2 Peter 1:3 and write down your thoughts on it.

_____
_____
_____
_____
_____
_____
_____
_____
_____

12. Conclusion

I want you to know I am on this journey with you. I feel like Paul when I say that I don't claim to have attained it but I press on toward full understanding of what it means to be a son of Father God and what it means to be invited to His table. It is a beautiful and wonderful thing that He has done and I am so deeply honored that He has brought me in so that I can reign with Him forever. I want to comprehend why He apprehended me.

I also want to be clear that by adopting us into His family, Father was only setting things in order. This adoption was not some plan B or some contrived way to get us back. We were always His. We were created in His heart. He did not separate from us, but rather it was us, and our rebellion against Him, that caused the separation. He was only taking back was always rightfully His!

I would like to tell you that I think all orphan nature or mentality has been completely removed from me, but I cannot. As I grow in Him and Holy Spirit reveals places that I don't trust Father or places of insecurity, I become keenly aware that there are traces of that orphan attitude trying to hang on. I don't stress or feel guilty, as that would be a waste of good emotions. Instead, I pull up to the table, prepared by my Father for me, even in the presence of my enemies, and I eat! I eat of the abundance of His house. I drink from His delightful streams. I drink deeply of grace and mercy and I rest in what He has done for me. He started the work, He will be faithful to complete it.

12. Conclusion

When He brings correction to me, I know He does so as a faithful Father. I rejoice to know He loves me enough to help me. He cares for me, as a loving Father should, and speaks tenderly to my heart, helping me to grow up. The writer of Hebrews addressed this aspect of sonship.

"Consider him who endured from sinners such hostility against himself, so that you may not grow weary or fainthearted. In your struggle against sin you have not yet resisted to the point of shedding your blood. And have you forgotten the exhortation that addresses you as sons? 'My son, do not regard lightly the discipline of the Lord, nor be weary when reproved by him. For the Lord disciplines the one he loves, and chastises every son whom he receives.'"

Hebrews 12:3-6

My Father loves me with an everlasting love. It was His lovingkindness that drew me to Him and it was that same lovingkindness that melted my heart, allowing me to trust Him. He has been a faithful Father and He has always been good.

Sometimes He took me around storms and showed me His miraculous power. Other times, we went right through the middle of the storm and He showed me His keeping power. No matter the situation, He has remained faithful and has brought me out of darkness into His marvelous light, just as He said He would do. His glory is so much more than I could have began to imagine it would be. His grace is deeper than I dared to believe in the beginning and His love is sweeter to me than anything earth can offer. What I experience with Him is beyond words. My human tongue and it's limited abilities cannot begin to describe what I have found Him to be. I so understand the hymn writer crying out in desperation, wishing that He had 10,000 tongues to sing God's praise. I too, feel that I am inadequate to even begin to explain what I have found in my Father's eyes.

12. Conclusion

He could have made me a slave in His Kingdom, an occupation that I would gladly have filled for eternity. He could have just built me a cabin on the outskirts of glory, like some sing about; I would have been forever filled with thanksgiving. He could have saved me just to serve Him for all the ages to come. But no, this was not His plan. He wanted me close. He wanted relationship. He wanted sons!

What kind of love is this? It is some amazing Agape, only God could have done this, kind of love! I am forever grateful. What He has purposed for us is so wonderful. What He has planned for us is beyond anything we have dared to believe; but Holy Spirit is revealing to us Father's heart and sons are awakening to it.

Recently, as I was looking at the story of David and Mephibosheth which I wrote about in Chapter Four, I saw something new. It causually mentions something toward the end of the story. Please understand that I have read and taught this story many times. I have used the whole story to describe grace because it is such a beautiful picture of love, mercy and covenant loyalties! However, this time I noticed a simple statement.

"And Mephibosheth had a young son, whose name was Mica. And all who lived in Ziba's house became Mephibosheth's servants. So Mephibosheth lived in Jerusalem, for he ate always at the king's table. Now he was lame in both his feet."

2 Samuel 9:12-13

Maybe you are as underimpressed by this as I was for years, but think about it for a moment. Even in his lame, fearful state, while being being plagued by an orphan mentality, hiding for his life, Mephibosheth has offspring. Even in that state, there was fruit in his life! You may feel like you

12. Conclusion

are too messed up to be used by God but I begged to differ with you. God can still do stuff in and through you, but it is not the same as being free and knowing your rights! When Mephibosheth was restored, it effected all those connected to him. His son, his fruit, now had what was rightfully his all along. But in order for that to happen, Mephibosheth had to come out of hiding and take his place at the kings table!

It is my prayer, now that you have read this book, that you are awakening to just how wonderful you are in Father's heart and just how special you are to Him. This is an amazing journey of discovery and recovery. You are discovering your true identity and recovering what was meant to be from the beginning. You are not an orphan. You are not abandoned. You have purpose and destiny and you are loved with an everlasting love!

Allow Holy Spirit to lead you into complete freedom. He is faithful to do His job. Remember, Jesus promised He would not leave us as orphans, but would send His Holy Spirit to bring us into the freedom of sonship. Do not grow weary. Again I say, do not grow weary! Trust the process that Holy Spirit is using and trust that He knows the end from the beginning and is working towards the Father's purpose. He is faithful and will finish what He has begun.

We are no longer orphans, we are SONS!